Reading & Writing
Great Wall of China

NATIONAL GEOGRAPHIC
LEARNING

Australia • Brazil • Mexico • Singapore • United Kingdom • United States

National Geographic Learning,
a Cengage Company

Reading & Writing, Great Wall of China

**Lauri Blass, Mari Vargo, Keith S. Folse,
April Muchmore-Vokoun, Elena Vestri**

Publisher: Sherrise Roehr

Executive Editor: Laura LeDréan

Managing Editor: Jennifer Monaghan

Digital Implementation Manager,
Irene Boixareu

Senior Media Researcher: Leila Hishmeh

Director of Global Marketing: Ian Martin

Regional Sales and National Account
Manager: Andrew O'Shea

Content Project Manager: Ruth Moore

Senior Designer: Lisa Trager

Manufacturing Planner: Mary Beth
Hennebury

Composition: Lumina Datamatics

Student Edition: Reading & Writing, Great Wall of China
ISBN-13: 978-0-357-13830-4

National Geographic Learning
20 Channel Center Street
Boston, MA 02210
USA

Locate your local office at **international.cengage.com/region**

Visit National Geographic Learning online at **ELTNGL.com**
Visit our corporate website at **www.cengage.com**

Printed in China
Print Number: 03   Print Year: 2020

PHOTO CREDITS

Scope and Sequence

Unit Title and Theme	Reading Texts and Video	ACADEMIC SKILLS Reading
1 **FOOD JOURNEYS** *page 1* ACADEMIC TRACK: Cultural Studies	**Reading 1** A Global Food Journey VIDEO Images of Greenland **Reading 2** Cooking the World	**Focus** Recognizing Pronoun References Predicting, Summarizing, Understanding Main Ideas and Details

Unit Title and Theme	Writing	Grammar for Writing
2 **OPINION PARAGRAPHS** *page 22*	What Is an Opinion Paragraph? Facts and Opinions Topic Sentences for Opinion Paragraphs Choosing a Topic for an Opinion Paragraph	Recognizing Word Forms and Common Suffixes

Unit Title and Theme	Reading Texts and Video	ACADEMIC SKILLS Reading
3 **HAPPINESS** *page 41* ACADEMIC TRACK: Health Science/Sociology	**Reading 1** Is There a Recipe for Happiness? VIDEO Longevity Leaders **Reading 2** Four Keys to Happiness	**Focus** Identifying the Main Idea Predicting, Understanding the Main Idea and Details, Matching, Identifying Main Ideas

Unit Title and Theme	Reading Texts and Video	ACADEMIC SKILLS Reading
4 **WHY WE BUY** *page 61* ACADEMIC TRACK: Business/Marketing	**Reading 1** The Psychology of Supermarkets VIDEO Who Do You Trust? **Reading 2** The Power of Persuasion	**Focus** Identifying Supporting Ideas Predicting, Understanding Main Ideas and Details, Understanding Purpose, Categorizing, Summarizing

VOCABULARY EXTENSION 76   GRAMMAR REFERENCE 79   BRIEF WRITER'S HANDBOOK 82

Critical Thinking	Writing	Vocabulary Extension
Focus Justifying Your Opinion	**Skill Focus** Paraphrasing Using Synonyms **Language for Writing** Giving Reasons **Writing Goal** Writing a paragraph explaining why people enjoy sharing pictures of food	**Word Forms** Words as Nouns and Verbs **Word Forms** Changing Adjectives into Adverbs

Building Better Vocabulary	Original Student Writing	
Word Associations Using Collocations	**Original Student Writing** Write an opinion paragraph. **Photo Topic:** Write your opinion about the best kinds of zoos. **Timed Writing Topic:** What minimum age should be required to get a driver's license?	

Critical Thinking	Writing	Vocabulary Extension
Focus Inferring Meaning from Context Justifying Your Opinion, Synthesizing, Reflecting	**Skill Focus** Writing a Strong Topic Sentence **Language for Writing** Review of the Simple Present Tense **Writing Goal** Writing an opinion paragraph about whether people in your community are happy	**Word Partners** Expressions with *living* **Word Forms** Words as Nouns and Verbs

Critical Thinking		Vocabulary Extension
Focus Relating Ideas Reflecting		**Word Partners** verb + *control* **Word Partners** *natural* + noun

FOOD JOURNEYS

1

**Freshly picked hyacinth beans,
West Bengal, India**

ACADEMIC SKILLS

READING	Recognizing pronoun references
WRITING	Paraphrasing using synonyms
GRAMMAR	Giving reasons
CRITICAL THINKING	Justifying your opinion

THINK AND DISCUSS

1 What do you see in the photo? Do people eat this kind of food in your country?

2 Skim through the unit. What types of food do you see?

A Read the information on these pages and answer the questions.

1. What do the photos show? Have you tried any food from these places?

2. Think about De Los Santos's questions for the photographers. Describe a picture that you might take to show these things.

B Match the words in blue to their definitions.

_____ (adj) usual or common; something you expect

_____ (v) to use or experience with others

_____ (n) the ideas or behavior of a people or society

THE WORLD ON A PLATE

Food photographer Penny De Los Santos believes that photos can tell powerful stories. So she gave photographers an assignment: Take a picture that shows the role of food in your **culture**.

De Los Santos told the photographers to think about the answers to these questions: What's a **typical** food scene in your world? What do your friends and family do when they eat together? How do they **share** meals?

De Los Santos received thousand of photos from photographers all over the world. She evaluated each one based on its color, lighting, composition (form), and story. Here are some of her favorites.

On a cold morning in Harbin, China, a woman prepares fresh steamed mantou (a bread-like bun).

A villager carries a tray of fruits and nuts during a festival in Iran.

Ingredients for brinjal curry, India

A family in Cambodia enjoys fresh pineapples.

Reading 1

PREPARING TO READ

BUILDING
VOCABULARY

A The words in blue below are used in the reading passage on pages 5–6. Read the paragraph. Then match the correct form of each word to its definition.

Many **types** of edible plants—plants you can eat—grow in Mediterranean countries such as Italy and Greece. Sometimes these plants—herbs, vegetables, and fruits—grow near people's homes. People often **pick** them, take them home, and use them right away. This way, they are still very **fresh**. One fruit in particular, the olive, grows well in the Mediterranean climate, so people use a lot of olive oil there. The oil has a good **taste**, so people often pour it right on their food. They also use it to **prepare** food. For example, if you visit a Mediterranean home, someone might **offer** you **fried** fish cooked in olive oil and a salad of fresh vegetables mixed with the oil.

1. _____ (v) to make something, such as food

2. _____ (n) a kind or a category

3. _____ (adj) cooked in fat, such as butter or oil

4. _____ (adj) recently made or produced; not old

5. _____ (v) to give something to someone

6. _____ (v) to take or remove something by breaking it off

7. _____ (n) flavor, e.g., fruity, sweet

USING
VOCABULARY

B Discuss these questions with a partner.

1. What **types** of edible plants grow where you live?

2. Do you eat a lot of **fried** food? Why or why not?

3. What kinds of food do you **offer** people when they come to your home?

BRAINSTORMING

C What are some typical dishes in your country or culture? Make a list and share your ideas with a partner.

1. _____ 2. _____ 3. _____

4. _____ 5. _____ 6. _____

PREDICTING

D The reading on pages 5–6 is about a trip that photographer Matthieu Paley made. Look at the photos and read the captions. Then discuss with a partner: What place is the passage mainly about? What kind of food do people eat there?

I think it's mainly about …
People probably eat … there.

A family in Crete gathers for lunch. The Mediterranean diet is one of the oldest diets still popular today.

A GLOBAL FOOD JOURNEY

🎧 Track 1

A In 2014, French photographer Matthieu Paley set out to explore the world of food. His travels took him through jungles, over mountains, and beneath the sea. He went on the journey to explore how our environment affects the food we eat—and how our diet[1] shapes our culture. Paley shared his experiences in a visual food diary, called *We Are What We Eat*.

B Paley saw how food plays an important role in people's lives all over the world. In Greenland, he went seal hunting with the Inuit to catch food for dinner. He gathered honey from trees with the Hazda people of Tanzania. And in Malaysian Borneo, he went diving to catch sea urchins[2] and octopuses.

C In Crete—the largest island in Greece—Paley enjoyed a typical Mediterranean family meal. On the following page is an excerpt from his diary.

During his journey, Paley visited six countries around the world to experience their food and culture.

[1] **diet:** the food that we often eat
[2] **sea urchin:** a small sea animal with a round shell and sharp spikes

I am at the Moschonas' home for their Saturday family gathering. Everyone was working in the fields this afternoon, and there is a pile of fresh wild herbs on the table. The family welcomes me, and the conversation is loud and lively. I feel right at home.

"Now, we make kalitsounia!" says Stella. These are small fried pies filled with wild herbs called horta. In Crete, April has been a time to pick horta for thousands of years. Stella prepares dough[3] on the table. She cuts it into small squares and wraps the herbs. Then she fries the little pies in olive oil.

Someone takes a large bucket of snails from the freezer. The Moschonas eat snails all year round. They are probably the oldest food eaten by humans. Snails may also be the easiest to catch, because you just go for a walk, turn over some rocks, and there they are.

[3]**dough**: a mixture of flour and water, often used for baking

"And they are full of Omega 3,[4] no fat on that meat either!" Stella says. She'll prepare the snails with a thick sauce. She offers me a kalitsounia, hot out of the pan.

"Tell me about the horta," I ask. "What did you pick today?"

Leaning over the table, Stella says with a smile, "Oh, there are over 20 types of herbs out there, if you know where to find them. And I know them all by name!"

My plate is filled with snails. On the table, there are also beans, small fried fish, and another vegetable. It looks like tiny asparagus, and has a bitter taste. Manolis sits next to me. He points at the dish. "This one is medicament. Medicine!" He says, "Eat a ton of it!" I try it. "We call these avronies … only in this season," he says. "You are a lucky man!"

[4]**Omega 3**: a type of fatty acid that is good for health

A typical Cretan meal of snails, sardines, and fava beans

UNDERSTANDING THE READING

A Complete the summary of the main ideas of the passage.

a. a diary
b. a typical Mediterranean meal
c. pictures
d. the food people eat
e. the world
f. to Crete

In 2014, Matthieu Paley went on a trip around ¹_____. He wanted to learn about the connection between ²_____ and where they live. Paley took ³_____ and kept ⁴_____ to record his experiences. In one entry, he described his visit ⁵_____, where he had ⁶_____.

B What does the writer express in the following paragraphs? Circle the best choice.

1. Paragraph D   why he traveled to Crete / how he felt at the dinner
2. Paragraph E   how Stella prepares kalitsounia / what kalitsounia tastes like
3. Paragraph F   a food with a long history / a dish with a strange taste
4. Paragraph J   Paley's meal at the Moschonas' / Paley's next food journey

C Match the types of food (1–5) with the descriptions. One type of food is extra.

_____ 1. kalitsounias   a. vegetables that look like small asparagus
_____ 2. horta   b. wild greens that people pick in April
_____ 3. snails   c. probably one of the oldest food people eat
_____ 4. fried fish   d. small pies filled with edible plants
_____ 5. avronies

> **CRITICAL THINKING**   **Justifying** means explaining the reasons for your opinion or preference. For example, when you evaluate something, think about why and how you made your decision.

D Look at the foods from Matthieu Paley's diary. How much would you like to try each one? Give each a number (1–3) and write a reason.

1 = I don't want to try it.   ⟶   3 = I really want to try it.

kalitsounia   1 2 3 _____

snails   1 2 3 _____

avronies   1 2 3 _____

Cretan kalitsounia

DEVELOPING READING SKILLS

READING SKILL Recognizing Pronoun References

Pronouns usually refer to nouns that appear earlier in a text. The pronoun may refer to a noun earlier in the same sentence or in a previous sentence.

A subject pronoun usually refers to a subject mentioned earlier.

Matthieu Paley set out on a food journey in 2014, and he visited six countries.
    subject   subject pronoun

Similarly, an object pronoun usually refers to an object mentioned earlier:

Someone took a bucket of snails from the freezer and put it on the table.
                 object   object pronoun

Note: Pronouns always match the nouns they refer to in number and in gender.

ANALYZING **A** Underline the subject and object pronouns in the following paragraph. Then draw an arrow to the noun that each pronoun refers to.

Food tourists travel just to explore food in different countries. When food tourists take a tour, they choose a place that has the type of food they want to explore. For example, food tourists might go to China and take cooking classes. Food experts might take the travelers to markets and help them buy fresh ingredients. In Mediterranean countries such as Spain and Italy, travelers can have farmhouse vacations. They stay on farms and learn about the local diet. They also help farmers pick fruit and vegetables and learn how to prepare them using local recipes.

IDENTIFYING PRONOUN REFERENCE **B** The sentences below are from the passage on page 6. Write the word(s) that each underlined pronoun refers to.

1. Paragraph **E**: Stella prepares dough on the table. <u>She</u> cuts <u>it</u> into small squares and wraps the herbs.

   She = _____   it = _____

2. Paragraph **F**: Snails may also be the easiest to catch, because you just go for a walk, turn over some rocks, and there <u>they</u> are.

   they = _____

3. Paragraph **I**: Leaning over the table, Stella says with a smile, "Oh, there are over 20 types of herbs out there, if you know where to find <u>them</u>. And I know <u>them</u> all by name!"

   them = _____   them = _____

4. Paragraph **J**: On the table, there are also beans, small fried fish, and another vegetable. <u>It</u> looks like tiny asparagus, and has a bitter taste.

   It = _____

Video

IMAGES OF GREENLAND

Isortoq, a village in east Greenland, has an average annual temperature of −1.3 °C, and a population of about 100 people.

BEFORE VIEWING

A Look at the photo caption and the title of the video. What do you think is a typical diet for someone living in this place? Discuss your ideas with a partner.

PREDICTING

B Read the information about Greenland and the Inuit culture. Then answer the questions.

LEARNING ABOUT THE TOPIC

The Inuit live in the Arctic regions of Greenland, Canada, and Alaska in the United States. Traditionally, they eat mostly meat because it is impossible to grow crops in the cold climates where they live. The Inuit eat seals, walruses, polar bears, birds, fish, and other Arctic animals. The traditional Inuit diet also includes some plants that grow naturally in the Arctic, such as roots, berries, and seaweed. Surprisingly, even though the traditional diet is 50–75% fat and does not include a lot of vegetables, the Inuit who eat this diet are very healthy. Today, most Inuit eat a combination of a traditional and a more modern diet because they have access to a variety of food in grocery stores.

1. How is a traditional Inuit diet different from your diet?

   _____

2. What shaped the traditional Inuit diet?

   _____

3. How has a typical Inuit diet changed in recent years?

   _____

The words in **bold** below are used in the video. Read the sentences. Then match the correct form of each word to its definition.

> Antarctica is one of the world's most **remote** places.
>
> Not many plants and animals can **survive** in places with extreme climates.
>
> **Hunting** seals and polar bears for food is part of the Inuit's traditional **lifestyle**.

1. _____ (n) way of living

2. _____ (v) to kill animals for food

3. _____ (adj) far away from everything

4. _____ (v) to continue to live even in difficult situations

WHILE VIEWING

A ▶ Watch the video. What was Matthieu Paley's main goal in Greenland? Circle the most suitable answer.

    a. to show the role that food plays in the Inuit culture

    b. to show how the Inuit diet is affected by modern lifestyles

    c. to learn about the effect fast food is having on the traditional Inuit diet

B ▶ Watch the video again. Put the events of Paley's experience in order (1–6).

_____ a. arrived in Isortoq

_____ b. spotted a seal's head in the ocean

_____ c. brought the seal back to the village

_____ d. went hunting with Magnus on a canoe

_____ e. went hunting with Bengt and Dina and caught a seal

_____ f. asked Dina if she could show him a real Arctic dish

AFTER VIEWING

A Which of Paley's Greenland photos do you remember best from the video? How would you describe it? Discuss your ideas with a partner.

_____

_____

B Note your answer to the question below. Then discuss with a partner.

Do you think Paley achieved his main goal? Why or why not?

_____

_____

Reading 2

PREPARING TO READ

A The words in **blue** below are used in the reading passage on pages 12–13. Complete each sentence with the correct word.

BUILDING
VOCABULARY

> A **dish** is a kind of meal or recipe.
>
> If something is **popular**, a lot of people like it.
>
> When you **argue** with someone, you disagree with them.
>
> A **recipe** is a set of instructions for making a type of food.
>
> When you **hope** to do something, you want and expect to do it.
>
> If you **respect** someone, you like them for their ability or knowledge.
>
> An **ingredient** is one of the things that you use to make a particular dish or meal.
>
> A **variety** is a group of things of a particular type that are all different in some way.

1. I _____ my grandfather for his patience and kindness.

2. Salt is an important _____. Cooks use it in almost every kind of

   _____ .

3. Some restaurants have secret _____ for making their food.

4. People often _____ on social media when they don't agree on a topic.

5. You can learn to cook a(n) _____ of dishes from food blogs.

6. If you _____ to create a(n) _____ blog, you should
   write about things that a lot of people are interested in.

B Discuss these questions with a partner.

USING
VOCABULARY

   1. Have you ever **argued** with people online?

   2. Do you know any trends that are **popular** online now?

C Why do you think people read food blogs? List three reasons. Then share your ideas
with a partner.

BRAINSTORMING

   1. _____

   2. _____

   3. _____

D The reading on page 12 is an interview with food blogger Sasha Martin. Look at the
title of the reading. What do you think Martin writes about in her blog? Check your
ideas as you read the passage.

PREDICTING

COOKING THE WORLD

🎧 Track 2

A Award-winning food writer Sasha Martin started her popular *Global Table Adventure* blog in 2010. Her plan was simple: to prepare a meal from every country in the world. Over the next four years, she cooked over 650 dishes from 195 countries. In this interview, Martin describes her experience of cooking the world.

Was "cooking the world" a way to travel without leaving home?

B That's right. I think the idea that exploration is for everyone is really important. There are so many people who dream of travel. But I think that you really can go on adventures without leaving home.

C With food, if you have the right ingredients, you can create the flavor of another place. It's like armchair travel, but it's faster and easier. I call it "stovetop travel."

What did you hope to teach your daughter by cooking the world?

D I wanted her to feel that she had a place in the world where she belonged. But I also feel it's important for children to grow up knowing people from other countries—their global neighbors.

E I call them neighbors because the world is so small now. I remember going on Facebook in its early days. I noticed there were people from different parts of the world commenting on posts, even arguing with each other. I feel that in that environment, young people need to be able to respect and understand each other.

So food is a great way to create that common ground?

F Yes. I wanted to share recipes that were bridges to other cultures. A lot of celebrity TV chefs tend to choose the most shocking recipes. But I think you need a bridge first. Then people won't put up a wall in their mind about that culture. They won't just think, "Gross[1]! Those people eat such weird[2] things!"

[1] gross: very unpleasant, disgusting   [2] weird: strange

One of Sasha Martin's recipes—Peruvian quinoa salad with olives and avocado

Sasha Martin and her daughter Ava

THE RISE OF THE FOOD BLOGGER

In July 1997, there was only one food blog on the Internet; today there are over two million. That first blog, *Chowhound*, was an online discussion board for sharing ideas about eating in New York. Today, food bloggers cover a wide variety of topics. Some examples:

- When Adam Roberts was in law school, he needed a break from studying. He decided to teach himself how to cook. Roberts started a blog to keep a record of his learning adventure and share it with other people. Eventually, his blog *The Amateur Gourmet* led to a new career in cooking.

- In May of 2012, two friends wanted to make each other laugh, so they created a blog for sharing pictures of ugly food. Other people began to send in their own photos of weird-looking food. By 2014, *Someone Ate This* was one of the Internet's most popular food blogs.

- A history student named Anje decided to share her love for history and cooking. On her websites, *Kitchen Historic* and *Food Roots*, readers can find dishes from the 13th century all the way to the 1980s.

UNDERSTANDING THE READING

UNDERSTANDING
MAIN IDEAS

A Check (✓) the three sentences that best describe Martin's blog and ideas.

☐ 1. Martin's blog provides a way to travel around the world without leaving home.

☐ 2. Martin's blog provides travel tips for making a journey around the world.

☐ 3. Martin thinks it's important for children to learn about other cultures.

☐ 4. Martin believes that food creates cultural connections.

☐ 5. Martin likes to include strange or unusual recipes on her blog.

UNDERSTANDING
DETAILS

B Why did each blogger create their food blog? Match each blogger to a reason or reasons (a–g).

> a. to make each other laugh
> b. to explore recipes from a long time ago
> c. to go on adventures without leaving home
> d. to help young people learn to respect each other
> e. to share a learning experience with people
> f. to share information about food in a particular city
> g. to teach her daughter and readers about other cultures

1. Sasha Martin _____

2. the creators of _____
   Chowhound

3. Adam Roberts _____

4. Anje _____

5. the creators of _____
   Someone Ate This

UNDERSTANDING
PRONOUN
REFERENCE

C Underline the pronouns in these sentences. Then draw an arrow to the noun that each pronoun refers to.

1. When Adam Roberts was in law school, he needed a break from studying.

2. Roberts started a food blog and shared it with other people.

3. In May of 2012, two friends wanted to make each other laugh, so they created a blog for sharing pictures of ugly food.

CRITICAL THINKING:
JUSTIFYING
YOUR OPINION

D How much would you like to read each blog? Rate each one (1–3), and give a reason for your choice.

1 = I'm not interested in it. ⟶ 3 = I would really like to read it.

Global Table Adventure	1 2 3	_____
Chowhound	1 2 3	_____
The Amateur Gourmet	1 2 3	_____
Someone Ate This	1 2 3	_____
Kitchen Historic / Food Roots	1 2 3	_____

Writing

EXPLORING WRITTEN ENGLISH

A Read the sentences below. Check (✓) the three sentences that give reasons. Then underline a word or phrase in each one that connects the reason and the result.

NOTICING

☐ 1. He went on a journey to explore how our environment affects the food we eat.

☐ 2. Sasha Martin started the popular *Global Table Adventure* blog in 2010.

☐ 3. I call them neighbors because the world is so small now.

☐ 4. It looks like tiny asparagus and has a bitter taste.

☐ 5. In May of 2012, two friends wanted to make each other laugh, so they created a blog for sharing pictures of ugly food.

LANGUAGE FOR WRITING Giving Reasons

Here are some words and phrases you can use to give reasons.

*Adam Roberts started a food blog **because** he needed a break from school.*
*Anje loves history and food, **so** she started a food blog.*
***One reason** (that) people start a blog is that they want to share their experiences.*
***Another reason** is (that) they want to improve their writing skills.*
*Some people start blogs **to** tell their friends about their daily lives.*

Notes:

• The reason comes before *so*, and the result follows it. A comma separates the two clauses.

• When an infinitive (*to* + base verb) is used to give a reason, *because*, a subject, and a verb can be left out in the reason clause.

   *Some people start blogs **(because they want) to tell** their friends about their daily lives.*

• You can switch the clauses in sentences with *because*. A comma separates the two clauses in this case:

   ***Because** he needed a break from school, Adam Roberts started a food blog.*

◀ One of the recipes Sasha Martin made was the German dessert baumkuchen, or "tree cake." It was given this name because the many layers inside look like the rings of a tree.

B Complete the sentences with a word or phrase for giving reasons.

1. De Los Santos asked photographers to take food pictures _____ she thinks it's a good way to learn about other cultures.
2. _____ people read Sasha Martin's blog is to find recipes. _____ is that they want to visit faraway places without leaving home.
3. Matthieu Paley took pictures of his travels _____ show the world typical food scenes from the places he visited.
4. People sometimes want to share their experiences, _____ they post photos of the food they eat.
5. Some chefs start food blogs _____ they want to write cookbooks.
6. Travelers often want to learn about local foods, _____ they read food blogs before they travel.

C Combine the sentences using a suitable word or phrase to make one sentence. There is more than one correct answer for some pairs of sentences.

1. Many people travel. They want to try new dishes.

   _____

2. In my opinion, *101 Cookbooks* is the best food blog. The photos are beautiful. The recipes are easy to follow.

   _____

   _____

3. Smartphones have good cameras. It's easy to take beautiful food pictures on a trip.

   _____

   _____

4. Paley wanted to show people the typical Arctic diet. He took pictures of a seal hunt.

   _____

   _____

WRITING SKILL Paraphrasing Using Synonyms

Paraphrasing is expressing the meaning of something using different words. One way of paraphrasing is using synonyms—words with a similar meaning—to avoid repeating the same word.

*Many people enjoy taking **photos** of **food**, but De Los Santos wanted more than just **pictures** of pretty **dishes**. She was also looking for great **photography**, so she used certain criteria for choosing the **images**.*

D Match each word with the best synonym (a–k).

1. _____ emotions   a. tasty
2. _____ typical   b. feelings
3. _____ role   c. upload
4. _____ believe   d. uninteresting
5. _____ photo   e. part
6. _____ post   f. usual
7. _____ fun   g. pretty
8. _____ delicious   h. dish
9. _____ beautiful   i. think
10. _____ boring   j. enjoyable
11. _____ food   k. picture

E Read the pairs of sentences below. Paraphrase the underlined part in each pair using synonyms. You can use the words in exercise D, or other words that you know.

1. Sasha Martin cooked dishes from all over the world. She <u>cooked dishes</u> from 195 different countries.

_____

_____

2. When Martin was young, she believed that cooking could be fun. As an adult, she still <u>believes</u> that <u>cooking</u> is <u>fun</u>.

_____

_____

3. Martin posts photos of her food online. Readers can <u>post</u> their own <u>photos</u> in the comments section of Martin's blog.

_____

_____

4. People often post photos of delicious and beautiful food that they cook. Other readers enjoy looking at the <u>photos</u> of the <u>delicious</u> <u>food</u>.

_____

_____

F Write a second sentence to follow each sentence below. Include a synonym of at least one of the words.

1. Matthieu Paley enjoyed a typical Mediterranean family meal in Crete.

_____

_____

2. Some people read food blogs because they want to get ideas for recipes.

_____

_____

WRITING TASK

GOAL You are going to write a paragraph on the following topic:

Explain why you think people like to share pictures of food on social media or on blogs. Give three reasons.

BRAINSTORMING **A** Read the list of reasons that people share photos of food on social media or on blogs. With a partner, brainstorm for more reasons.

They want to …
- tell people about a great meal that they ate
- tell people that they're eating healthy food
- get cooking advice
- give food or restaurant reviews

- _____
- _____
- _____

PLANNING **B** Follow these steps to make notes for your paragraph. Don't worry about grammar or spelling. Don't write complete sentences.

Step 1 Decide whether you are going to write about the sharing of food on social media or on blogs. Write a topic sentence.

Step 2 Look at your brainstorming notes. Rank your reasons and choose the top three. Write them in the outline as your supporting ideas.

Step 3 Add at least one detail for each reason.

OUTLINE

Topic sentence: _____

Supporting Idea 1: _____

_____

Detail: _____

Supporting Idea 2: _____

_____

Detail: _____

Supporting Idea 3: _____

_____

Detail: _____

FIRST DRAFT **C** Use the information in your outline to write a first draft of your paragraph.

REVISING PRACTICE

The drafts below are similar to the one you are going to write, but they are on a different topic:

Explain why you think people should try food from different cultures. Give three reasons.

What did the writer do in Draft 2 to improve the paragraph? Match the changes (a–d) to the highlighted parts.

a. added a detail for a supporting idea
b. used a synonym
c. deleted unrelated information
d. added a word or phrase that introduces a reason

Draft 1

I believe that it is important for people to try food from different cultures. They will learn about other countries. When they research recipes for food from other countries and try new ingredients, they will discover new things about those places. It's important to follow a recipe when you are cooking something new. Also, people should try foreign foods because they can experience a country without actually going there. It can be expensive to travel to a foreign country, but it's easy and inexpensive to try a dish from that country. Finally, I think people should try food from other cultures to make cooking and eating more enjoyable.

Draft 2

I believe that it is important for people to try food from different cultures. One reason is that they will learn about other countries. When they research recipes for food from other countries and try new ingredients, they will discover new things about those places. Also, people should try foreign foods because they can experience a country without actually going there. It can be expensive to travel to a foreign country, but it's easy and inexpensive to try a dish from that place. Finally, I think people should try food from other cultures to make cooking and eating more enjoyable. Eating the same dishes all the time is boring, and trying different types of food can be an adventure.

D Now use the questions below to revise your paragraph.

REVISED DRAFT

☐ Did you use suitable words and phrases to introduce reasons?

☐ Did you include a detail for each supporting idea?

☐ Did you use synonyms to avoid repetition?

☐ Do all your sentences relate to the main idea?

EDITING PRACTICE

Read the information below.

In sentences with words and phrases that show reasons, remember:
- that the reason comes before *so*, and the result comes after it.
- that in sentences with *so*, a comma separates the two clauses.
- to separate the two clauses with a comma when you begin a sentence with *because*.
- that in an infinitive, the base form of the verb always follows *to*.

Correct one mistake with language for introducing reasons in each of the sentences (1–6).

1. Some people want to share their good eating habits so they post pictures of their meals on social media.

2. I think people post pictures of the food they make to sharing their hobby with their friends.

3. Food blogger Clotilde Dusoulier quit her job so she wanted to become a full-time food writer.

4. Because they want to make some money some food bloggers have ads on their sites.

5. People read food blogs, because they need ideas for things to make for dinner.

6. Some people post pictures of their food to tells people about new restaurants in town.

FINAL DRAFT **E** **Follow these steps to write a final draft.**

1. Check your revised draft for mistakes with language for introducing reasons.

2. Now use the checklist on page 81 to write a final draft. Make any other necessary changes.

UNIT REVIEW

Answer the following questions.

1. What is one thing you learned in this unit about food in a different culture?

_____

_____

_____

2. What are two words or phrases you can use to introduce a reason?

_____

_____

3. Do you remember the meanings of these words? Check (✓) the ones you know. Look back at the unit and review the ones you don't know.

Reading 1:

☐ culture AWL   ☐ fresh   ☐ fried

☐ offer   ☐ pick   ☐ prepare

☐ share   ☐ taste   ☐ type

☐ typical

Reading 2:

☐ argue   ☐ dish   ☐ hope

☐ ingredient   ☐ popular   ☐ recipe

☐ respect   ☐ variety

NOTES

Giant panda Wei Wei walks around
a birthday cake made of fruits and
bamboo in Wuhan Zoo.

OBJECTIVES To learn how to write an opinion paragraph
To practice writing facts and opinions
To recognize word forms and common suffixes

Can you write your opinion about the best kinds of zoos?

What Is an Opinion Paragraph?

An **opinion** paragraph expresses the writer's thoughts and attitiude toward something. The writer attempts to persuade the reader about a certain point of view. In other words, the writer presents an argument for or against something. This kind of writing is also referred to as persuasive or argumentative writing.

Good writers will include not only opinions but also facts to support their opinions. For example, if a writer says "Smoking should not be allowed anywhere," he or she must give reasons for this opinion. One reason could be a fact, such as, "Over 160,000 people died in the United States last year because of lung cancer as a known result of smoking." This fact clearly and strongly supports the writer's opinion.

A good opinion paragraph:

- is often about a controversial issue
- gives the writer's opinion or opinions about a topic
- explains facts to support the writer's opinions
- presents a strong case that makes the reader think about an issue seriously, perhaps even causing the reader to reconsider his or her own opinion about the issue
- considers both sides of an argument (although it gives much more attention to the writer's side of the issue)

ACTIVITY 1 **Studying Example Opinion Paragraphs**

Discuss the Preview Questions with your classmates. Then read the paragraphs on pages 24–28 and answer the questions that follow.

Opinion Paragraph 1

This paragraph is about cell phone use while driving, which has been a topic of much interest and debate in many countries for some time.

Preview Questions

1. Do you think that using a cell phone while driving is acceptable? Why or why not?

2. Should there be laws banning the use of cell phones while driving? Why or why not?

Example Paragraph 1

Driving and Cell Phones

Because cell phones and driving are a **deadly** mix, I am in favor of a ban on all cell phone use by drivers. The most **obvious** reason for this ban is to save lives. Each year thousands of drivers are killed or seriously injured because they are talking on cell phones or texting instead of watching the road while they are driving. This first reason should be

deadly: dangerous, able to cause death

obvious: evident, clear

enough to support a ban on cell phones when driving, but I have two other reasons. My second reason is that these drivers cause accidents that kill other people. Sometimes these drivers kill other drivers; sometimes they kill passengers or even pedestrians. These drivers certainly do not have the right to **endanger** others' lives! Finally, even in cases where there are no **injuries** or deaths, **damage** to cars from these accidents costs us millions of dollars as well as countless hours of lost work. To me, banning cell phones while driving is **common sense**. In fact, a **wide range of** countries has already put this ban into effect, including Australia, Brazil, Japan, Russia, and Turkey. Driving a car is a privilege, not a right. We must all be careful drivers, and talking or texting on a cell phone when driving is not safe. For the important reasons I have mentioned here, I support a complete ban on all cell phone use by drivers.

to endanger: to cause to be in a dangerous situation

an injury: harm or hurt done to a body (for example, a foot)

the damage: harm or hurt done to thing (for example, a building)

common sense: so obvious that everyone knows it

a (wide) range of: a (great) number of

Post-Reading

1. What is the topic sentence of the paragraph? _____

_____

2. What is the author's opinion on cell phone usage by drivers? _____

_____

3. List three reasons that the writer favors a ban on cell phones while driving.

a. _____

b. _____

c. _____

4. What is your reaction to this paragraph? Do you agree or disagree with the author's opinion? Why or why not?

_____

_____

_____

Opinion Paragraph 2

This paragraph is about a less serious topic than the topic that Example Paragraph 1 deals with. The subject of this paragraph is the question "Which is better, calling or texting?"

Preview Questions

1. How many phone calls do you make each day?

2. How many text messages do you send each day?

3. Do you prefer to call or text someone when you need to tell that person something? Why?

Example Paragraph 2

The Best Way to Communicate

No matter how much my friends try to convince me that I should text them more often, I prefer calling to texting. Yes, some people might say that using a telephone to make a call is **old-fashioned**, but I do not care. Texting is certainly very common now because it is convenient and fast. However, I really like to call my friends because I want to hear my friends' voices and interact with them. **Without a doubt**, calling is my preferred **mode of** communication.

no matter: it does not matter or make a difference

old-fashioned: old style, not modern

without a doubt: 100 percent, certainly

a mode: a method, manner

Post-Reading

1. What is the topic sentence of this paragraph? _____

_____

2. What phrases from the paragraph show the reader that the writer is giving an opinion and not a fact?

_____

_____

3. Do you agree with the supporting statements that the writer makes about texting and calling? Why or why not?

_____

_____

_____

4. Can you think of at least one other reason the writer could give for preferring calling to texting?

_____

_____

Opinion Paragraph 3

The paragraph on the next page deals with school uniforms, a current controversial issue.

Preview Questions

1. Have you ever worn a school uniform?

2. Do you think requiring students to wear a uniform is a good idea or a bad idea?

An A+ for School Uniforms

School uniforms should be **mandatory** for all students for a number of important reasons. First of all, uniforms make everyone equal. In this way, kids with a lot of nice things can be on the same level as those with fewer things. In addition, getting ready for school every morning can be much faster and easier. Many kids waste time choosing what to wear to school, and they and their parents are often unhappy with their final choice. Most important, some **studies** show that school uniforms make students **perform** better in school. Some people might say that uniforms take away personal freedom, but students still have many other ways to express themselves and their individuality. For all these reasons, I believe the benefits of mandatory school uniforms are so strong that we should require them immediately.

mandatory: obligatory, something that must be done

a study: a research report

to perform: to produce work; to do

Post-Reading

1. What is the author's opinion about school uniforms?

   _____

   _____

2. The author gives three reasons to support the opinion. Write them here.

   _____

   _____

   _____

3. The paragraph states that some people do not think that school uniforms should be required. What is their main reason?

_____

_____

Writer's Note

Advanced Opinion Writing

The most important way to persuade someone to agree with what you are writing is to include strong supporting facts. Your writing will always sound better when you support what you have just written with evidence or good examples.

A second way to persuade someone to agree with the ideas in your writing is to include at least one sentence with an opposing opinion (an opinion that disagrees with your point of view). At first, this might not seem like a good idea, but it is common to state one point of view that disagrees with your own point of view. This is called a **counterargument.** This counterargument is then followed by a statement that refutes, or reduces the counterargument. This is called a **refutation** because you refute the counterargument.

When you acknowledge this other opinion, you should downplay, or minimize, it. One way to do this is to use weak words, such as _some, may,_ and _might,_ as we can see in the following example:

> Some people **might** say that uniforms take away personal freedom, but students still have many other ways to express themselves and their individuality.

In a good opinion paragraph, the writer:

- states an opinion about a topic

- provides supporting sentences with factual information

- briefly mentions one opposing point of view (the counterargument)

- refutes the counterargument in one or two sentences (the refutation)

- finishes the paragraph with a concluding sentence that restates the topic sentence and/or offers a solution. Study this example:

State your opinion ⟶	Without a doubt, all high school students **should** be
Give a counterargument ⟶	required to volunteer in their community. **While some may claim that** students should focus solely on their
Refute it ⟶	studies during school hours, **research has actually found** that volunteering improves students' motivation both in
Give your Supporting Fact for your Opinion #1 ⟶	and out of the classroom. **In a recent poll** by the student council, 71 percent of students who volunteered were
Give your Supporting Fact for your Opinion #2 ⟶	better able to manage their time and grades. **Furthermore, students at Western High School have overwhelmingly reported** that they felt like they were part of something greater and could see how their efforts could truly help
State your conclusion ⟶	those around them. **Based on** all of the research and results, schools **should** require students to volunteer.

Facts and Opinions

A **fact** is information that can be verified or proved. A fact is always true. In contrast, an **opinion** is what someone thinks or believes to be true. An opinion may be true or false.

Facts	Opinions
Orlando is located in central Florida.	Orlando is a great city for people of all ages.
Orlando is home to several large theme parks.	There are many fun places to visit in Orlando.
The University of Central Florida is located in Orlando.	The University of Central Florida is an excellent university.
The average annual temperature is 73° F.	I like the weather in Orlando very much.

When you write an opinion paragraph, it is very important to include facts. If you choose helpful supporting facts with examples that the reader can clearly relate to, your opinion paragraph will be stronger and you may even convince readers to agree with you. Readers will remember good, related supporting examples, so you should try to write the most convincing examples.

ACTIVITY 2 Identifying Facts and Opinions

Read the following statements and decide if they are facts or opinions. Write F for fact and O for opinion.

___O___ 1. Soccer is a much more interesting game to play and watch than golf.

___F___ 2. The Nile River splits into the White Nile and Blue Nile in Sudan.

_____ 3. The most beautiful city in the world is Paris.

_____ 4. Citrus fruits include oranges, lemons, and grapefruit.

_____ 5. Hawaii is the best place for a vacation.

_____ 6. The capital of Thailand is Bangkok.

_____ 7. Security alarms are the most effective way to protect homes from burglaries.

_____ 8. School uniforms should be mandatory for all students.

_____ 9. A glass of milk has more calcium in it than a glass of apple juice.

_____ 10. Apple juice tastes better than milk.

Reread Example Paragraph 1 about cell phone use while driving. It contains some information that is factual and some that is the writer's opinion. Find two examples of facts and two examples of opinions in the paragraph and write them on the lines below.

Fact

1. _____

_____

2. _____

_____

Opinion

1. _____

_____

2. _____

_____

Topic Sentences for Opinion Paragraphs

A good topic sentence for an opinion paragraph must express an opinion that can be supported in some way. Therefore, this type of topic sentence cannot be a fact because a fact is not an opinion. A fact does not need to be proved or discussed. It is a fact. If you cannot think of at least two good reasons to support the idea in the topic sentence, then it is probably not a good topic sentence for an opinion paragraph.

Bad Topic Sentence: Paris is a large city in France.

Problem: This is a fact. Does anyone disagree that Paris is a large city and it is in France?

Bad Topic Sentence: There are several types of camels.

Problem: This is a fact. This topic sentence is going to produce a paragraph explaining the different kinds of camels, but it is not a good topic sentence for an opinion paragraph about camels.

ACTIVITY 4 **Recognizing Good Topic Sentences for Opinion Paragraphs**

Read the following sentences. Which ones are good topic sentences for opinion paragraphs? Put a check (✓) next to those sentences.

_____ 1. A hospital volunteer usually has many duties.

_____ 2. Soccer is a much more interesting game to play and watch than golf.

_____ 3. The largest and best-known city in all of France is Paris.

_____ 4. Eating a vegetarian diet is the best way to stay healthy.

_____ 5. Hawaii is the best place for a vacation.

_____ 6. The U.S. government uses a system of checks and balances.

_____ 7. Although Ontario is the fourth largest of the thirteen provinces in Canada, it has about one-third of Canada's population and is therefore the most populated province in the entire country.

_____ 8. Security alarms are the most effective way to protect homes from burglaries.

ACTIVITY 5 **Sequencing Sentences in a Paragraph**

The following sentences make up a paragraph. Read the sentences and number them from 1 to 6 to indicate the correct order. Then write O or F on the line after each sentence to indicate whether the sentence contains an opinion or a fact.

_____ a. The damage of these rays may not be seen immediately in children, but adults who spent a lot of time in the sun when they were children have a much higher chance of developing skin cancer than adults who did not spend time in the sun. _____

_____ b. Too much time in the sun can cause severe skin damage, especially in young children. _____

_____ c. This disease, which can be deadly if it is not treated quickly, is a direct result of the sun's harmful ultraviolet rays. _____

_____ d. In conclusion, the information in this paragraph is enough evidence to persuade parents not to let their children play outside in the sun without sunscreen. _____

_____ e. Although many people enjoy playing in the sun, parents should make sure that their children put on sunscreen before going outside. _____

_____ f. The most serious example of this is skin cancer. _____

Now copy the sentences from Activity 5 in the best order to create a good opinion paragraph. Add a title of your choice.

Example Paragraph 4

_____

_____

_____

_____

_____

_____

_____

_____

_____

_____

_____

Grammar for Writing

Recognizing Word Forms and Common Suffixes

Many English words have different forms for different parts of speech—**noun, verb, adjective, or adverb.** Some words have **suffixes** or endings that indicate the part of speech. Notice the suffixes in these parts of speech:

Part of Speech	Purpose	Common Suffixes		Examples
Noun	Names a person or thing	-ion	vacation	In this photo, you can see the **beauty** of a sunset.
		-ment	entertainment	
		-er	teacher	
		-ness	sadness	
		-ity	activity	
		-ence	difference	
Verb	Shows action or being	-ify	classify	The city will **beautify** several neighborhoods.
		-ize	realize	
		-en	blacken	
		-ate	generate	
Adjective	Describes or modifies a noun	-ful	beautiful	That is the most **beautiful** baby I've ever seen.
		-ent	different	
		-able	comfortable	
		-ish	English	
		-ial	financial	
		-y	windy	
Adverb	Modifies a verb, adjective, or another adverb	-ly	quickly	Susan sings **beautifully.**
			extensively	

Sometimes a word can function as different parts of speech without any change in ending. For example, the word *paint* can be a noun *(Where is the paint?)* or a verb *(Let's paint the kitchen.)*. The word *hard* can be an adjective *(The candy is hard.)* or an adverb *(She studied hard.)*. Always check your writing for the correct word forms.

ACTIVITY 7 Identifying Word Forms

Each item below contains a group of related words. Identify the word form of the words in each group. Write N (noun), V (verb), ADJ (adjective), or ADV (adverb) on the line. (Some items will not have all four forms.) Use a dictionary if necessary.

1. increasingly ___ADV___
   increase ___N___
   increasing ___ADJ___
   increase ___V___

2. believe _____
   belief _____
   believable _____

3. legality _____
   legal _____
   legally _____
   legalize _____

4. logically _____
   logic _____
   logical _____

5. finance _____
   financially _____
   finance _____
   financial _____

6. sweetly _____
   sweetness _____
   sweet _____
   sweeten _____

7. simplicity _____
   simply _____
   simple _____
   simplify _____

8. equality _____
   equal _____
   equalize _____
   equally _____

9. benefit _____
   beneficial _____
   beneficially _____
   benefit _____

10. freedom _____
    freely _____
    free _____
    free _____

ACTIVITY 8 Correcting Word Forms

Some of these sentences contain word form errors. Read each sentence. If the sentence is correct, write C on the line. If it contains an error, write X on the line and correct the word form error.

1. _____ Many people did not belief the world was round before Christopher Columbus's voyages.

2. _____ She parked her car illegally and got a $30 ticket.

3. _____ Taking multivitamins can be benefit to your health.

4. _____ Students in this class are allowed to speak freedom.

5. _____ During civil rights demonstrations, protesters fought for equality.

6. _____ Babies often speak using simply words and phrases.

7. _____ My sister is a very sweetly girl.

8. _____ Mathematicians must use their logical to solve difficult problems.

9. _____ Taxpayers do not want the government to increase taxes.

10. _____ The company's financial situation has improved dramatically this year.

Choosing a Topic for an Opinion Paragraph

To help you choose a topic for your paragraph, you should first **brainstorm**. **Brainstorming** is quickly writing down all thoughts that come into your head. When you brainstorm, you do not think about whether the idea is good or bad or whether your writing is correct. The process is called brainstorming because it feels like there is a storm in your brain—a storm of ideas.

A good method of brainstorming is to make two **columns** about your topic. On one side, list the negative ideas about the topic; on the other side, list the positive ideas.

Here is an example of how to set up a negative-positive brainstorm design.

TOPIC:	
Negative Points	Positive Points

When you write an opinion paragraph later in the unit, try to make a list of all of the positive and negative points of a topic. It will help you decide which points will make the strongest opinion or argument.

Building Better Vocabulary

ACTIVITY 9 **Word Associations**

Circle the word or phrase that is most closely related to the word or phrase on the left. If necessary, use a dictionary to check the meaning of words you do not know.

	A	B
1. obvious	serious	evident
2. mandatory	possible	required
3. a report	to study	to do again

4. to set up	to design, plan	to change, alter
5. a point of view	an opinion	permission
6. to split	to combine	to divide
7. to ban	to prohibit	to transport
8. severe	negative	positive
9. without a doubt	it is certain	it is possible
10. an injury	an advantage	a problem
11. to downplay	to maximize	to minimize
12. duties	fun	work
13. entirely	annually	completely
14. a voyage	a trip	a subject
15. to convince	to persuade	to restate

ACTIVITY 10 **Using Collocations**

Fill in each blank with the word or phrase on the left that most naturally completes the phrase on the right. If necessary, use a dictionary to check the meaning of words you do not know.

1. but also / for example   not only X, _____ Y

2. for / from   to protect your home _____ burglaries

3. all / no   first of _____

4. agree / offer   to _____ a solution

5. in / on   to spend money _____ food

6. may / than   rather _____

7. communication / effort   a method of _____

8. damage / evidence   to cause _____

9. fact / issue   a controversial _____

10. doing / to do   to waste time _____ something

Original Student Writing: Opinion Paragraph

ACTIVITY 11 **Original Writing Practice**

Develop a paragraph about a strong opinion that you have. Include facts to support your opinion. Follow these guidelines:

- Choose a topic such as the value of living abroad, connecting teachers' salaries to students' grades, or why young children need their own cell phones.

- Brainstorm your topic. If you want, use the Internet for ideas.

- Write a topic sentence with a controlling idea.

- Write supporting sentences with facts that support your opinions.

- Check for incorrect word forms.

- Use at least two of the vocabulary words or phrases presented in Activity 9 and Activity 10. Underline these words and phrases in your paragraph.

If you need ideas for words and phrases, see the Useful Vocabulary for Better Writing on pages 111–115.

ACTIVITY 12 **Peer Editing**

Exchange papers from Activity 11 with a partner. Read your partner's paragraph. Then use Peer Editing Sheet 1 on ELTNGL.com/sites/els to help you comment on your partner's paragraph. Be sure to offer positive suggestions and comments that will help your partner improve his or her writing. Consider your partner's comments as you revise your own paragraph.

Additional Topics for Writing

Here are some ideas for opinion paragraphs. When you write, follow the guidelines in Activity 11.

PHOTO TOPIC: Look at the photo on pages 22–23. In your opinion, what are the best kinds of zoos?

TOPIC 2: Do you think professional athletes receive too much money? Why or why not?

TOPIC 3: Should students have to take an entrance exam to enter a college or university? Why or why not?

TOPIC 4: Should schools last all year?

TOPIC 5: Who is the person that you admire the most? Give reasons for your choice.

Timed Writing

How quickly can you write in English? There are many times when you must write quickly such as on a test. It is important to feel comfortable during those times. Timed-writing practice can make you feel better about writing quickly in English.

1. Take out a piece of paper.

2. Read the writing prompt.

3. Brainstorm ideas for five minutes.

4. Write a short paragraph (six to ten sentences).

5. You have 25 minutes to write.

In many places, the minimum age necessary to obtain a driver's license is 16 or 17. Many people say this minimum age should be increased to 21. In your opinion, what minimum age should be required to get a driver's license?

NOTES

HAPPINESS

3

A group of children play inside a jeepney in Cebu City, Philippines.

ACADEMIC SKILLS

READING Identifying the main idea
WRITING Writing a strong topic sentence
GRAMMAR Review of the simple present tense
CRITICAL THINKING Inferring meaning

THINK AND DISCUSS

1 What does it mean to be happy?
2 Think of someone you know who seems happy. Describe that person.

A Look at the information on these pages and answer the questions.

1. Have you been to any of the countries shown here? Why do you think people from these countries are happy?

2. Compare the information about these six countries. Do you see a strong link between GDP per capita and overall happiness? What does this suggest?

B Match the correct form of the words and phrases in blue to their definitions.

_____ (v) to supply or make available

_____ (adj) protected from danger or harm

_____ (n) the level of comfort and amount of money that people have

5 CANADA
Rating: 8.0

Population: 35.5 million
Average Life Expectancy:
82.0 years
GDP per capita:
$50,440

Population: 124.2 million
Average Life Expectancy:
76.7 years
GDP per capita:
$10,450

HAPPY HOT SPOTS

What makes us happy? According to the World Database of Happiness, people are happy if they feel that they have a good quality of life. This may include having a good **standard of living**, feeling safe and **secure**, or living in a society that **provides** basic healthcare for all.

Is it possible to measure happiness? Researchers at the World Database of Happiness think so. The database (2005–2014) brings together scientific reports on happiness from 158 countries around the world. The researchers asked people to rate their enjoyment of life on a scale from 0 to 10. The top six happiest nations are shown here. Oman (18th) is the happiest country in the Middle East. The happiest Asian countries—the Philippines, Thailand, and Singapore—placed 39th, 42nd, and 43rd.

4 **ICELAND**
Rating: 8.1

Population: 327,400
Average Life Expectancy:
82.9 years
GDP per capita:
$52,470

2 **DENMARK**
Rating: 8.4

Population: 5.6 million
Average Life Expectancy:
80.7 years
GDP per capita:
$62,430

1 **COSTA RICA**
Rating: 8.5

Population: 4.8 million
Average Life Expectancy:
79.4 years
GDP per capita:[1]
$10,650

✚

6 **SWITZERLAND**
Rating: 8.0

Population: 8.2 million
Average Life Expectancy:
83.2 years
GDP per capita:
$85,800

[1] **GDP (Gross Domestic Product) per capita** is the value of goods and services produced by a country, divided by its total population.

Reading 1

PREPARING TO READ

BUILDING
VOCABULARY

A The words and phrases in **blue** below are used in the reading passage on pages 45–46. Complete each sentence with the correct word or phrase. Use a dictionary to help you.

> access   basic necessities   equal   financial   freedom   poverty   socialize

1. When you _____, you spend time with other people for fun.

2. Countries with high levels of _____ should put more social programs in place to help the poor.

3. According to a United Nations report, having _____ to the Internet is a basic human right.

4. If you ask someone for _____ advice, you are concerned about money.

5. People who do the same job should receive _____ pay.

6. _____ of speech is a basic democratic value.

7. In some of the world's poorest countries, obtaining _____ like clean water and shelter is a daily struggle.

USING
VOCABULARY

B Discuss these questions with a partner.

1. Who do you normally **socialize** with?
2. Besides food and shelter, what do you think are the **basic necessities** in life?
3. Is **poverty** a serious problem in your country? If so, what is the government doing to tackle this problem?

BRAINSTORMING

C List six things that you think a person needs in order to be happy. Share your ideas with a partner.

1. _____   3. _____   5. _____

2. _____   4. _____   6. _____

PREDICTING

D Look at the title and the subheads of the reading passage on pages 45–46. What do you think the reading passage is about? Check your answer as you read.

a. how to measure happiness
b. things that make people happy
c. life in the happiest country in the world

▲ Families in Singapore often gather to eat in open-air hawker centers.

IS THERE A RECIPE FOR HAPPINESS?

🎧 Track 3

A What makes us happy? Money? Friends? A good job? Are the answers the same for everyone? According to world surveys, Mexico and Singapore are two happy countries—but their people may be happy for different reasons.

SAFETY AND SECURITY

B There are more than 21,000 people per square mile[1] in the small nation of Singapore. People on the island work very long hours and regularly bring work home with them. The country has strict laws against smoking in public, littering,[2] and even jaywalking.[3] But according to the World Database of Happiness, Singapore is one of the happiest countries in Asia. Why?

C One reason for Singapore's happiness is that the government provides the basic necessities, such as housing and healthcare. There is almost no extreme poverty in Singapore. The government "tops up"[4] poorer people's incomes so everyone can have a minimum standard of living. It also offers tax breaks[5] to people who look after their aging parents. The result is a lot of closely connected families with roughly equal standards of living.

D People may not be happy about all the laws, but they are generally happy with the results— they breathe clean air, they don't step in litter, and the streets are safe and orderly. So for Singaporeans, it seems that living in a secure,

[1] A **square mile** = 2.59 square kilometers.
[2] **Littering** is leaving trash lying around outside.
[3] **Jaywalking** occurs when a pedestrian walks across a street at a place where it is not allowed.

[4] If you **top** something **up**, you add to it to make it full.
[5] If the government gives someone a **tax break**, it lowers the amount of tax they have to pay.

clean, and safe place may be more important than having a lot of personal freedom. Many societies are trying to find a happy medium between order and freedom. Singapore's ranking on the World Database of Happiness suggests that the country has done a pretty decent job at it.

FRIENDS AND NEIGHBORS

In many ways, Mexico is the opposite of Singapore. There are some parts of Mexico where people do not have a safe or secure life. Many people do not have jobs, enough food, or access to education. But, as in Singapore, most people in Mexico feel that they are happy. Why?

One reason is the importance of social interaction. According to psychologists, much of our happiness comes from feeling that we are part of a larger community. Simple acts like smiling at a neighbor or having dinner with friends can greatly increase our overall happiness. People in Mexico socialize with family and friends a lot, and this adds to their happiness.

But what about poverty? In Mexico, about half of the population is poor. However, most Mexicans live near people in a similar financial situation. If your neighbor doesn't have expensive items—such as a big house or an expensive car—you probably don't feel the need to have those things either. So money, by itself, may not be that important for happiness. What matters more is how much money you have compared to the people around you.

A MIXED RECIPE?

So the question "What makes people happy?" does not seem to have a simple answer. Security, safety, freedom, and socializing with friends and family can all play important roles. As the examples of Singapore and Mexico suggest, there may be no single recipe for happiness. It is up to each of us to find our own.

Festive gatherings and parades help create a strong sense of community in Mexico.

UNDERSTANDING THE READING

A What is the main idea of the reading passage?

UNDERSTANDING
THE MAIN IDEA

   a. Happiness means different things to different people.

   b. Personal freedom is the most important thing for happiness.

   c. Everyone needs to feel safe and secure in order to be happy.

B According to the writer, do the following statements (a–e) apply to Mexico, Singapore, or both? Complete the Venn diagram.

UNDERSTANDING
DETAILS

   a. Most people here feel that they are happy.

   b. People generally feel safe and secure.

   c. Family connections are important for people's happiness.

   d. Although many people here are poor, most of them are happy.

   e. Most people accept the government's strict rules as part of life.

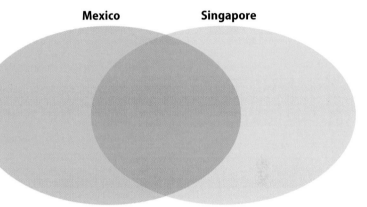

Mexico   **Singapore**

CRITICAL THINKING   Use the context—the words around a word—to **infer**, or guess, the **meaning** of vocabulary you don't know. The context can also help you decide the word's part of speech (e.g., noun, verb, or adjective). For example:

The government "tops up" poorer people's incomes so everyone can have a minimum standard of living.

We can guess from this context that *minimum* is probably an adjective used to describe the least or smallest amount required.

C Find and underline the following **bold** words and phrases in the reading passage. Use context to identify their meanings. Then match each word or phrase to its definition.

CRITICAL THINKING:
INFERRING
MEANING

strict (paragraph B)   **happy medium** (paragraph D)

look after (paragraph C)   **decent** (paragraph D)

1. _____ (v) to take care of someone or something

2. _____ (adj) tough; must be obeyed

3. _____ (adj) good enough; satisfactory

4. _____ (n) a good choice or condition that avoids any extremes

D Would you prefer to live in Singapore or Mexico? Why? Complete the following sentence and share your ideas with a partner.

CRITICAL THINKING:
JUSTIFYING YOUR
OPINION

I think I would prefer to live in **Singapore / Mexico** because _____

_____

DEVELOPING READING SKILLS

READING SKILL Identifying the Main Idea

The main idea of a paragraph is the most important idea, or the idea that the paragraph is about. A good paragraph has one main idea and one or more supporting ideas. Read the paragraph below and think about its main idea.

Researchers have found that the sunny weather in Mexico is one of the reasons that people there are happy. Mexico has many hours of sunlight, so people in Mexico get a lot of vitamin D. Vitamin D is important for overall health and well-being. Also, studies show that when people tan, they make more endorphins—chemicals in our bodies that make us feel happy.

Which of these statements is the main idea of the paragraph?

a. *People in Mexico are happy because they get a lot of vitamin D.*

b. *Tanning makes us create more endorphins, which make us feel happy.*

c. *Mexico gets a lot of sun, which may make people there happier.*

The last sentence is the main idea. The other two sentences are supporting ideas that explain the main idea.

MATCHING **A** Look back at the reading passage on pages 45–46. Match each main idea below to a paragraph (A–H) from the reading passage.

_____ 1. One reason people are generally happy is that the government provides financial support to the poorer members of society.

_____ 2. You don't need to have a lot of money to be happy.

_____ 3. Spending time with family and friends can contribute to happiness.

_____ 4. There are different answers to the question, "What makes people happy?"

_____ 5. Most people are willing to give up certain freedoms to gain more safety and stability.

IDENTIFYING THE MAIN IDEA **B** Read the information about Denmark. Then write the main idea of the paragraph.

It's hard to be happy when you're unhealthy. According to the 2014 World Database of Happiness, Denmark is the second happiest country in the world, and most Danes are fit. They have a lower rate of obesity than many of their European neighbors. Danish cities are designed so it's easy to walk or cycle from one place to another. For instance, many roads in Copenhagen have a special lane just for cyclists. And with a 30-minute walk, you can go from the city of Copenhagen to the ocean, where you can sail or swim, or to the woods, where you can hike. Everyone has easy access to recreation.

Main Idea: _____

_____

Video

Tonino Tola, a shepherd from Sardinia, stays active by taking care of his land.

LONGEVITY LEADERS

BEFORE VIEWING

A Some people live 100 years or more. What do you think these people do to stay healthy? Discuss your ideas with a partner.

PREDICTING

B Read the information about achieving a long life. Then answer the questions.

LEARNING ABOUT THE TOPIC

In some countries, people are living very long lives. Some are even living beyond 100. What are some of their secrets to longevity? Scientific research shows that eating the right foods plays a big role in determining how long you'll live. A healthy diet includes plenty of fruit, vegetables, and low-fat dairy products. Exercise is also important. A study published in *PLOS Medicine* found that people who exercised at recommended levels gained 3.4 years of life compared to those who were inactive. In addition, research suggests that there is a link between happiness and lifespan—happy people with a positive outlook on life tend to live longer and experience better health than their unhappy peers.

1. What are three things people do that increases their lifespan?

   _____

2. Why do you think there is a connection between happiness and longevity?

   _____

C The words and phrases in **bold** below are used in the video. Match the correct form of each word or phrase to its definition.

> A significant number of Japanese people live very long lives. There are almost 52 **centenarians** per 100,000 people in Japan.
>
> **Processed foods**, such as frozen pizza, aren't good for your health.
>
> Some elderly people prefer to live a **traditional lifestyle**. For example, they eat the same kinds of food their ancestors ate.

1. _____ (n) a way of living that is based on old customs

2. _____ (n) a person who lives to be 100 years old or older

3. _____ (n) food that has been altered from its natural state and that contains added chemicals

WHILE VIEWING

A ▶ Watch the video. According to the video, which of the following is true?

a. The world will struggle to meet the needs of an aging population.
b. Happiness is the most important factor in determining longevity.
c. Both medical science and lifestyle choices can help improve longevity.

B ▶ Watch the video again and answer the questions below.

1. What is one reason the world population is expected to increase in the future?

_____

2. What is one animal that can live a very long time? How long can it live for?

_____

3. What are two characteristics of Okinawa's centenarians that lead to good health?

_____

4. Describe one way younger Okinawans are different from the centenarians.

_____

AFTER VIEWING

A Discuss these questions with a partner.

1. Are there a lot of elderly people in your community? Why do you think this is?
2. In the video, the narrator says, "Some scientists have started to treat aging as a disease instead of a natural part of human life." What do you think this means?

B Compare Okinawa with either Singapore or Mexico. What is one thing people in those places have in common? Complete the following sentence.

People in Okinawa and _____ are generally happy because _____

_____

Reading 2

PREPARING TO READ

BUILDING VOCABULARY

A The words in **blue** below are used in the reading passage on pages 52–53. Complete each sentence with the correct form of the word. Use a dictionary to help you.

mood	community	volunteer	factor
support	long-term	grateful	well-being

1. A person's _____ goals can include saving money for retirement.

2. In some _____, adult children _____ their elderly parents financially by paying their medical and household bills.

3. Healthy food, exercise, and interpersonal relationships are important for a person's physical and mental _____.

4. Many people _____ to help those who were affected by the earthquake. The victims were very _____ for the help they received.

5. A person's _____ can change depending on the weather. For example, _____ such as sunlight and higher temperatures can make you feel happier.

USING VOCABULARY

B Discuss these questions with a partner.

1. How would you describe your **community**? What is it like to live there?
2. What are some things that put you in a good **mood**?

BRAINSTORMING

C The reading passage on pages 52–53 looks at four basic factors for happiness. Write the factors in the word web below. Then, with a partner, brainstorm some words or phrases that you think might relate to each one.

Happiness

FOUR KEYS TO HAPPINESS

A group of Japanese men enjoy a meal outdoors.

Researchers have found that different people need different things to be happy. But there are some basic things that anyone can do to become happier. Here are four areas of your life you can focus on to improve your long-term happiness.

1. STAY CONNECTED

Psychiatrist Robert Waldinger directs the Harvard Study of Adult Development, one of the longest-running studies of adult behavior. The study tracked the lives of two groups of men in the United States for over 75 years. One of the main findings from the study is the importance of social connections. "It turns out that people who are more socially connected to family, to friends, to community, are happier," says Waldinger. "They're physically healthier, and they live longer than people who are less well-connected." The happiest people meet regularly with friends and family, and support each other in difficult times.

2. KEEP ACTIVE

Nic Marks is the founder of the Happy Planet Index, which tracks national well-being around the world. One of the most important ways to improve well-being, he believes, is to keep active—healthy people are happier people. "The fastest way out of a bad mood," Marks says, is to "step outside, go for a walk, turn the radio on and dance. Being active is great for our positive mood." Being close to nature can also boost happiness. "Our pleasures are really ancient," says psychologist Nancy Etcoff. "We have a response to the natural world that's very profound." Walking a pet in the outdoors, for example, can improve our mood. Pets not only encourage their owners to be healthy, they also provide love and friendship, increasing their owners' self-esteem.

3. BUY LESS

The amount of money you have is a factor for happiness—but your salary may be less important than how you use it. Think carefully before buying expensive clothes or a new car, for example. Try to spend money instead on things that will really enrich your life, such as music lessons, or a vacation with family or friends. "We need to think before we buy," urges designer Graham Hill, and "ask ourselves: 'Is that really going to make me happier?'" Too often we buy things we don't really need. The less stuff we have in our lives, Hill argues, the happier we will be.

4. GIVE AWAY

Social science researcher Michael Norton has studied happiness levels around the world. He found that the act of giving money to people has a powerful effect on the giver as well as the receiver. "Almost everywhere we look," says Norton, "we see that giving money away makes you happier than keeping it for yourself." The amount of money isn't so important. "What really matters is that you spent it on somebody else rather than on yourself," he adds. Another way to give away is to donate your time instead of money. People who volunteer at homeless shelters, for example, find that it helps take the focus off their own problems and makes them feel grateful for what they have. Author David Steindl-Rast believes that being grateful may be the most important foundation for happiness: "It is not happiness that makes us grateful. It's gratefulness that makes us happy."

UNDERSTANDING THE READING

A Which sentence best summarizes the reading passage?

a. There are four different types of happy people in the world.
b. There are some small changes everyone can make to increase happiness.
c. Forming social connections is more important for happiness than other factors.

B Read the six scenarios below. Check (✓) the four that follow the advice in the reading passage.

☐ 1. A student installs a budget app on her phone to help control her spending.
☐ 2. A woman offers to take her neighbor's dog for a walk each morning.
☐ 3. A man uses all his savings to pay for an expensive new sports car.
☐ 4. A teenager spends time each Saturday helping at a children's hospital.
☐ 5. A young woman decides to reduce her number of working hours each week.
☐ 6. An elderly man decides to join an art class at a community center.

C Find and underline the **bold** words and phrases below on pages 52–53. Use context to identify their meanings. Then circle the correct answers to complete the definitions.

1. If you have high **self-esteem**, you feel (*confident / unsure*) about yourself.

2. **Salary** is the amount of (*work / money*) that an employee receives.

3. To **enrich** something means to make it (*better / last longer*).

4. If you **take the focus off** something, you give it (*more / less*) attention.

D Choose three factors from the reading passage that you feel are most important for happiness. Write a sentence for each one describing how you can change that area of your life to become happier. Then share your ideas with a partner.

Example: *Keep Active—I can go swimming every week.*

1. _____

_____

2. _____

_____

3. _____

_____

Writing

EXPLORING WRITTEN ENGLISH

A Read the sentences below. Which describe general facts and which describe routines? Circle **F** for fact or **R** for routine.

NOTICING

1. There are more than 21,000 people per square mile in the small nation of Singapore.   F   R

2. I work an average of 50 hours per week.   F   R

3. The government offers tax breaks to people who look after their aging parents.   F   R

4. Most people in Mexico live near people in a similar financial situation.   F   R

5. My friends and I go to the gym three times a week.   F   R

6. They have lunch together every day.   F   R

7. Iceland is one of the happiest countries in the world.   F   R

8. We usually cycle to work.   F   R

9. She reports to her boss once a month.   F   R

LANGUAGE FOR WRITING Review of the Simple Present Tense

We use the simple present tense to talk about facts or things that are generally true.

*About 5.6 million people **live** in Singapore.*

*There **are** over seven billion people in the world today.*

*Singapore **doesn't have** a high level of poverty.*

We also use the simple present tense to talk about habits and daily routines—things we do regularly, or things we usually don't do.

*They **walk** to work every day.*

*On most weekends, she **volunteers** at the homeless shelter.*

*I **don't see** my friends on Sundays.*

For simple present tense verbs, we use the base form with *I, you, we,* and *they.* We add *-s* to the base form for third-person singular subjects.

Some verbs have irregular present tense forms:

be: *I am; he/she/it is; you/we/they are*

do: *I/you/we/they do; he/she/it does*

have: *I/you/we/they have; he/she/it has*

To form a negative statement, use *doesn't* or *don't* and the base form of the verb.

B Underline the simple present tense verbs in the sentences in exercise A.

C Complete the sentences using the simple present tense of the verbs in parentheses.

1. According to researchers, happy people _____ (spend) a lot of time socializing with family and friends.

2. People in my office _____ (be) generally happy because the company _____ (offer) a good work-life balance.

3. In Denmark, the government _____ (provide) free healthcare and education to its citizens. Everyone _____ (have) equal access to basic necessities.

4. When people _____ (not / feel) safe in their neighborhood, they generally _____ (not / be) very happy.

5. Centenarians in Okinawa and Sardinia _____ (have) similar lifestyles— they _____ (grow) their own vegetables and _____ (eat) natural foods.

D Using the simple present tense, write three sentences about things you do regularly that make you feel happy.

1. _____

_____

2. _____

_____

3. _____

_____

E Using the simple present tense, write three sentences that describe general facts about your country or community.

1. _____

_____

2. _____

_____

3. _____

_____

Most paragraphs include a sentence that states the main idea of the paragraph. This sentence is called the topic sentence. It is usually the first sentence in the paragraph, but not always. Topic sentences can also appear within the paragraph or at the end of the paragraph.

A strong topic sentence should introduce the main idea of the paragraph. It should not be too general or too specific. For example, if the paragraph is about how the government helps increase people's happiness, this idea should be included in the topic sentence.

Singaporeans are generally happy. → **weak topic sentence; too general**

One reason Singaporeans are generally happy is that the government provides basic necessities, such as housing. → **strong topic sentence**

As another example, if the paragraph presents the argument that you don't need a lot of money to be happy, this idea should be included in the topic sentence.

About 50 percent of Mexico's citizens live in poverty. → **weak topic sentence; too specific**

Even though many people in Mexico live in poverty, overall reported happiness is still very high. → **strong topic sentence**

F Underline the topic sentence in each paragraph. One of the topic sentences is stronger than the others.

1. In Mexico, family is important. Family members are very close and support one another during difficult times. Grandparents take care of grandchildren so the children's parents can go to work and earn money. When the children grow up, they take care of their parents. This is one of the reasons why people in Mexico are generally happy.

2. Studies have shown that laughter may be an important factor for happiness and that people who laugh a lot are happier. People who laugh more tend to have higher levels of self-esteem. They also tend to be healthier. Laughter is so important for our general well-being that some people go to "laughter therapy," where they laugh with groups of other people.

3. It's important to like your job. In many countries, a lot of people choose their job based on how much it pays or on what other people think about that job. But in Denmark, one of the world's happiest countries, most people take jobs that interest them. That gives them a better chance to feel motivated and happy at work.

G Rewrite the two weak topic sentences from exercise F.

1. _____

_____

2. _____

_____

WRITING TASK

GOAL You are going to write a paragraph on the following topic:

Do you think people in your community are generally happy or unhappy? Give three reasons for your answer.

BRAINSTORMING **A** Brainstorm a list of things that make people in your community happy and a list of things that people in your community may be unhappy about.

Things people in my community are happy about	Things people in my community are unhappy about

PLANNING **B** Follow these steps to make notes for your paragraph.

Step 1 Look at your notes above. Do you think people in your community are generally happy or unhappy? Write a topic sentence in the outline below.

Step 2 Choose three things from your notes above that support your topic sentence. Note them in the outline as reasons.

Step 3 For each reason, write one or two details, examples, or facts. Don't worry about grammar or spelling. Don't write complete sentences.

OUTLINE

Topic: Are people in your community generally happy or unhappy?

Topic Sentence: _____

Reason 1: _____

Detail(s): _____

Reason 2: _____

Detail(s): _____

Reason 3: _____

Detail(s): _____

FIRST DRAFT **C** Use the information in your outline to write a first draft of your paragraph.

REVISING PRACTICE

The drafts below are similar to the one you are going to write, but they are on a different topic:

Are you generally happy or unhappy? Describe three things that make you happy or unhappy. Write two or more details about each one, and explain why it makes you feel this way.

What did the writer do in Draft 2 to improve the paragraph? Match the changes (a–d) to the highlighted parts.

a. corrected a verb form
b. added details to explain a reason
c. deleted unrelated information
d. made the topic sentence stronger

Draft 1

I think I'm generally happy. I has a great job. I do work that I feel passionate about, and I like my co-workers. I don't make a lot of money, so sometimes I have to do extra work on the weekends. I want to ask for a raise at work. My family and friends are very supportive. Whenever I have problems, I know that my family and friends will help me. My friends also make me laugh a lot. In addition, I'm healthy.

Draft 2

I think I'm generally happy because I like most things about my life. I have a great job. I do work that I feel passionate about, and I like my co-workers. My family and friends are very supportive. Whenever I have problems, I know that my family and friends will help me. My friends also make me laugh a lot. In addition, I'm healthy. I don't have any illnesses, and I play fun sports such as soccer and basketball.

D **Now use the questions below to revise your paragraph.**

REVISED DRAFT

☐ Does the paragraph have one main idea?

☐ Does a strong topic sentence introduce the main idea?

☐ Does the paragraph include three reasons that relate to the main idea?

☐ Does the paragraph include one or two details for each reason?

☐ Are all verb forms correct?

☐ Is there any information that doesn't belong?

EDITING PRACTICE

Read the information below.

In sentences using the simple present tense, remember to:

- use the correct verb endings with third-person singular subjects; for example, *he likes*, *she walks*.
- watch out for verbs that have irregular forms in the simple present: *be*, *have*, and *do*.
- use the correct form of *do* and the base form of a verb in negative statements; for example, *don't spend / doesn't spend*.

Correct one mistake with the simple present tense in each sentence below.

1. I enjoy the work that I do because it's very challenging, but I doesn't like my boss.

2. My co-workers are supportive, friendly, and fun, and I enjoying spending time with them after work.

3. It's important to me to spend time with my family members, but it's difficult because they don't lives close to me.

4. Although my house is not big and fancy, my neighborhood are very safe.

5. My friends and I exercises together every day to stay healthy, and that contributes to our happiness.

6. My grandfather is still very active and spend a lot of time outdoors.

7. Most happy people has hobbies like hiking or playing a musical instrument.

FINAL DRAFT   **E**   **Follow these steps to write a final draft.**

1. Check your revised draft for mistakes with simple present verb forms.

2. Now use the checklist on page 81 to write a final draft. Make any other necessary changes.

UNIT REVIEW

Answer the following questions.

1. Of the factors for happiness you learned about in this unit, which one do you think is most important?

_____

_____

2. When do you use the simple present tense?

_____

_____

3. Do you remember the meanings of these words? Check (✓) the ones you know. Look back at the unit and review the ones you don't know.

Reading 1:

☐ access AWL   ☐ basic necessities   ☐ equal

☐ financial AWL   ☐ freedom   ☐ poverty

☐ provide   ☐ secure AWL   ☐ socialize

☐ standard of living

Reading 2:

☐ community AWL   ☐ factor AWL   ☐ grateful

☐ long-term   ☐ mood   ☐ support

☐ volunteer AWL   ☐ well-being

WHY WE BUY

4

Colorful advertisements along
a shopping street in Tokyo

ACADEMIC SKILLS

READING   Identifying supporting ideas
CRITICAL THINKING   Relating ideas

THINK AND DISCUSS

1   What kind of advertisements do you most
    commonly see? Where do you see them?

2   How many advertisements do you think you
    see in a day?

A **Read the information on these pages and answer the questions.**

1. What kind of advertising do most companies in the United States do?

2. What advertising method is more effective in getting people to spend money?

B **Match the words in blue to their definitions.**

_____ (n) one part of 100

_____ (n) something that is made for sale

_____ (v) to believe someone or something

A WORLD
OF ADS

According to a 2014 study, a typical adult in the United States sees a few hundred advertisements—or ads—a day. These ads appear in a variety of ways: on posters, in magazines, on TV, and on the Internet. Among these, online advertising is the most popular way of reaching people. Companies in the United States are now spending more money on online ads than TV ads.

However, people seem to trust TV ads more than ads that they see on social media sites. A media organization in the United States reports that 37 percent of television viewers make buying decisions after watching TV ads, compared to 7 percent of people who buy a product after seeing ads on social media.

A huge ad covers the
wall of a clothing store
in Moscow.

Reading 1

PREPARING TO READ

BUILDING VOCABULARY **A** The words in blue below are used in the reading passage on pages 65–66. Read the paragraph. Then match the correct form of each word or phrase to its definition.

In 1994, Pizza Hut launched a website that allowed customers to order a pizza online **instead of** calling a restaurant. The first pizza ordered in this way was one of the first examples of online shopping. Since then, the number of online **stores** has grown quickly. Online shopping is an **attractive** option for many people: it allows them to shop at any time of the day and **avoid** crowds. In 2015, there were 1.46 billion online shoppers— about 20 percent of the world's population. And that figure continues to rise.

1. _____ (adj) nice, appealing

2. _____ (prep) in place of, as another option

3. _____ (n) a place where you can buy things

4. _____ (v) to stay away from something

BUILDING VOCABULARY **B** Read the sentences in the box. Then match the words in blue to their definitions.

> You can **control** the amount of money you spend by creating a savings plan.
>
> As society moves away from using **cash** and toward electronic payments, more people are comfortable with shopping online.
>
> Companies always need to improve their sales **strategies** in order to do better than their competitors.

When you …

1. **control** something, _____
2. pay in **cash**, _____
3. think of a **strategy**, _____

a. you give money in the form of coins and bills.
b. you make a plan for getting the best results.
c. you are able to do what you want with it.

USING VOCABULARY **C** Discuss these questions with a partner.

1. When do you usually pay in **cash**? When do you use other forms of payment?
2. What kinds of things do you buy online? What do you prefer to buy in a **store**? Why?

PREDICTING **D** Work with a partner. Think about where you can find the following items in a supermarket: milk, fruit and vegetables, and candy. Why do you think supermarkets put these items in those places? Check your ideas as you read the passage.

Solutions

WE LOVE FOOD

THE PSYCHOLOGY OF SUPERMARKETS

▲ Supermarkets are designed to make people spend more money.

🎧 Track 5

A When we go shopping at a supermarket, we often buy more than we need. But it may not be our fault—supermarkets are controlling the way we shop. In fact, the whole experience of shopping for food is planned and arranged for us. Every detail of a supermarket has a purpose. The way the aisles are organized, the music, the lighting, the product advertising—all these things make us stay longer and spend more.

B From the moment we enter, a supermarket's floor plan controls the way we experience the store. There is usually only one way in and one way out, so we have to start and stop at particular places. Fruit and vegetables and the bakery are usually near the entrance. Fresh produce and the smell of bread baking can make a store seem fresh and attractive. This puts us in a good mood and makes us hungry, so we take our time and buy more food.

In addition, we often have to walk through the whole supermarket to find what we need. For example, common items that most people shop for—like milk and eggs—are usually at the back of the store. Popular items are often placed in the middle of aisles, so we have to walk through the aisles to get what we want. Supermarkets also put expensive food at eye-level where they are easy to reach. Cheaper items are placed on lower shelves, so we have to bend down to get them. Cash registers are usually at the exit, so we have to walk through the entire store before getting to the payment area. All of these strategies make us see more food and spend more money.

Supermarkets use other techniques to control our shopping experience, too. For example, they play music to affect how we shop. In a study of shopping habits in a New York City supermarket, researchers found that slow music in a store makes us shop more slowly. In fact, when supermarkets play slow music instead of fast music, shoppers spend about 38 percent more. Additionally, most grocery stores don't have any clocks or windows. We can't look outside or see what time it is while we shop. That way, we don't know how long we've been shopping.

So what can you do to avoid buying more than you need? First, make a list and don't buy anything that isn't on it. If you don't trust yourself to do this, bring only enough cash to buy what you need. Second, don't shop too often. Plan several days of meals and shop for food only once or twice a week. Lastly, don't shop when you're hungry. That's when everything in the store looks delicious!

▼ Sometimes, supermarkets encourage shoppers to buy food by giving them samples to try.

UNDERSTANDING THE READING

A What is the main idea of the reading passage?

a. It has become more difficult for supermarkets to attract shoppers in recent years.

b. Supermarkets use certain methods to make shoppers spend more money.

c. There are some ways supermarket shoppers can avoid spending too much money.

B According to the reading, where are the following items usually placed? Note them on the diagram.

> milk   fruit and vegetables   expensive cereal   cash registers   cheap cereal

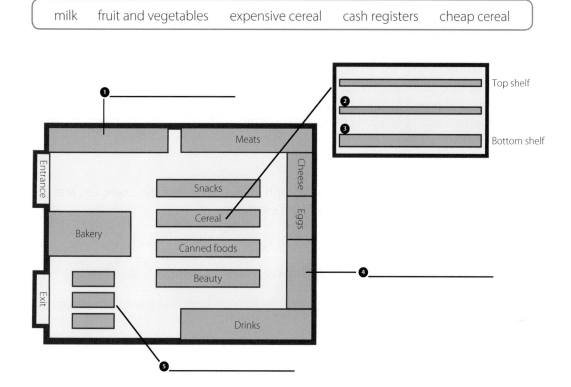

C Match the items in **B** to the reasons for where they are placed in a supermarket.

_____ 1. milk
_____ 2. cash registers
_____ 3. cheap cereal
_____ 4. expensive cereal
_____ 5. fruit and vegetables

a. to make the store front attractive
b. to make it easier to see and reach
c. to make it more difficult to reach
d. to make customers walk to the back of the store
e. to make customers walk through the entire store

> **CRITICAL THINKING** As you read, try to **relate** the information to your own experience. Ask yourself: What information about the topic does the writer give? Does it match my own experience or situation?

D What's your local supermarket like? In what ways is it similar to or different from the one described? What do you think are the reasons for the differences? Discuss with a partner.

DEVELOPING READING SKILLS

READING SKILL Identifying Supporting Ideas

Supporting ideas tell the reader more about the main idea of a paragraph. They can give specific examples of what the main idea means. They can also be reasons that explain the examples.

Read the following paragraph:

From the moment we enter, a supermarket's floor plan controls the way we experience the store. There is usually only one way in and one way out, so we have to start and stop at particular places. Fruit and vegetables and the bakery are usually near the entrance. Fresh produce and the smell of bread baking can make a store seem fresh and attractive. This puts us in a good mood and makes us hungry, so we take our time and buy more food.

The blue sentence gives an example—**what** the design of supermarkets is usually like and **how** it controls the way people experience the store. The green sentences give reasons to support the example—**why** supermarkets are designed in that way.

IDENTIFYING
SUPPORTING IDEAS

A Read the topic sentence in the paragraph below. Underline the examples, and double underline the reasons that support the examples.

Supermarkets use various strategies to get customers to buy their products.

One way is placing products for children on lower shelves. This makes it easier

for children to see and then ask their parents to buy something. Another strategy

is giving out free food samples. Seeing, tasting, and smelling food can make people

feel hungry and want to buy it. Supermarkets also place candy and other cheap items

at the registers as customers might buy a snack while they wait in line.

CATEGORIZING

B Is each sentence below a main idea or a supporting idea in the reading passage on pages 65–66? Write **M** for Main Idea or **S** for Supporting Idea.

1. The whole experience of shopping for food is planned and arranged for us.   _____

2. Cheaper items are placed on lower shelves, so we have to bend down to get them.   _____

3. Supermarkets use other techniques to control our shopping experience, too.   _____

4. In fact, when supermarkets play slow music instead of fast music, shoppers spend about 38 percent more.   _____

Video

WHO DO YOU TRUST?

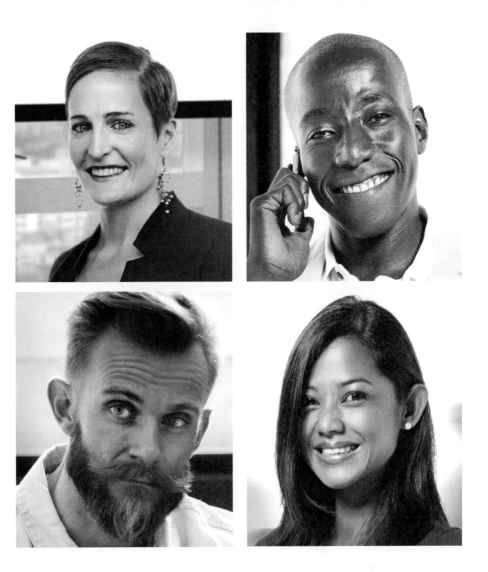

BEFORE VIEWING

A Look at the photos. Who do you think has the most persuasive face? Why? Discuss your ideas with a partner.

ANALYZING

B Read the information about Alex Todorov. Then check (✓) the sentences that Todorov is likely to agree with. Discuss your answers with a partner.

LEARNING ABOUT THE TOPIC

Psychology professor Alex Todorov studies how people make decisions. He's especially interested in how we evaluate people's personalities. He believes that people often make decisions about another person just by looking at their face. For example, we may decide whether or not the person is friendly, or whether we can trust them. Todorov's research also shows that people make these evaluations very quickly—in less than a second.

☐ 1. Our first impressions are usually influenced more by what people say than what they look like.

☐ 2. People usually decide within a short time if they will like someone.

☐ 3. When we see someone we don't know, we create an idea of them based on their appearance.

C The words in **bold** below are used in the video. Read the paragraph. Then match the correct form of each word or phrase to its definition.

One thing employers often want to know about a job seeker is if they are **competent** enough to do a good job. They also usually want to know if a person is **trustworthy**—whether or not you can depend on them. So how do they decide on the best person for the job? Experts say employers often make **judgments** just by looking at **candidates**. It's therefore important that job seekers present themselves well at the beginning of interviews, because people can form first impressions **in the blink of an eye**.

1. _____ (adj) honest; reliable

2. _____ (n) a decision

3. _____ (adv) very quickly

4. _____ (n) a person applying for a position

5. _____ (adj) having the necessary skills or qualities

WHILE VIEWING

A ▶ Watch the video. What does the experiment in the video show?

a. Most people are able to recognize smiles that aren't real.

b. Most people can guess the winner of an election by looking at their face.

c. Most people feel that what a politician does is more important than how they look.

B ▶ Watch the video again. Complete the sentences by circling the correct options.

1. According to Todorov, winning political candidates usually looked like they were _____.

   a. sociable and persuasive   b. skilled and honest

2. Todorov found that people seemed to trust people with faces that looked more _____.

   a. female   b. male

3. The experiment suggests that sometimes we may _____.

   a. make judgments based on feelings more than reason

   b. be able to tell whether someone is lying by looking at their face

AFTER VIEWING

A Did you choose the correct candidate each time? What helped you make your choices? Discuss with a partner.

B Work with a partner. Describe a time when your first impresssion of someone was inaccurate. What made you change your mind about them?

Reading 2

PREPARING TO READ

A Read the definitions of the words in **blue**. Then complete the sentences with the correct form of the words.

> Something that is **natural** is not man-made.
>
> A **customer** is a person who buys something.
>
> If something is **probably** true, it is very likely to be true.
>
> When you **notice** something, you see or become aware of it.
>
> A person's **attitude** toward something is how they think and feel about it.
>
> A **message** is the main meaning of something that a person writes or says.
>
> If you can **influence** people, you can make them think a certain way.
>
> When there is a **limit** on something, there is a fixed level or amount allowed.

1. Successful businesses know how to attract _____.

2. Credit cards have a(n) _____ on the amount of money you can spend with them.

3. Positive online reviews can change people's _____ toward a certain product and _____ them to buy it.

4. A common _____ in advertisements is that a product is effective.

5. This product contains only _____ ingredients, so it's _____ good for your health.

6. Many shopping malls don't have windows, so people may not _____ how much time they spend in there.

B Discuss these questions with a partner.

1. Is there an interesting ad that you **noticed** recently? What was it?
2. What are some ways ads try to make people remember their **message**?

C Read the title and the first paragraph of the passage on pages 72–73. What do you think the passage is about? Then check your answer as you read.

a. the importance of colors in product advertising
b. how advertising affects our shopping decisions
c. a comparison of various advertising strategies

THE POWER
OF PERSUASION

ADVERTISING STRATEGIES

- **Emotional Impact [3]:** Advertisers try to persuade us that their product will make us feel better, such as making us more attractive or loved.
- **Celebrity [4] Power:** Advertisers know that if we see a famous person using a product, we're more likely to buy it.
- **The Perfect Family:** Ads with happy families enjoying a product send a message: we can have the perfect family, too, if we buy the product.

CELEBRATE

A bus passes by an ad for the movie *Shrek*.

GREAT
JUNE ISSUE O

A You're shopping, and you see two similar products. How do you decide which one to buy? You might think you make this decision by yourself—but this isn't always the case.

Don't believe it? Try this. What word is missing?

APPLE   TREE   GRASS   GR_____

B What was the first word you thought of? Did you think of "green"? That's probably because we influenced your answer. The words "tree" and "grass" made you think of the color green, right? The color of the words also influenced your decision. This is an example of priming.

C Psychologist Joshua Ackerman explains that priming is a way to "use cues[1] to influence your attitudes [and] responses, often without you even noticing." Priming speeds up our decision-making. That's why advertisers use it to persuade us to buy things.

INFLUENCING YOUR THINKING

D Use of color is one type of priming. Did you ever notice that a lot of signs and packaging use the color red? Studies show that red gives people warm and positive feelings. We feel good about products connected with the color red, so we want to buy them. Green, on the other hand, makes products seem natural. Food companies often use green packages to make their food seem healthy.

E Descriptions in ads and signs also influence buying decisions. For example, studies show that if an ad says there's a limit to the number of items you can buy, you'll want more of them. Why? According to psychologists, something becomes more attractive if it's rare.

F The sounds in ads also influence decision-making. For example, advertisers sometimes use rhymes[2] in their ads. In a study at the University of Texas, researchers showed people pairs of messages with the same meaning—one that rhymed and one that didn't. The study found that people are more likely to believe the rhyming message. Rhymes are also easier for people to remember, so when they go shopping, they're more likely to buy the product.

G Advertisers use a lot of techniques to persuade customers to buy their products. You might think you're in control when you shop, but maybe you're not. Priming strategies could be influencing your decisions.

[1]**cues:** signs or signals that tell you to do something
[3]**emotional impact:** If something has emotional impact, it affects the way you feel.
[2]**rhyme:** a set of words with similar sounds
[4]**celebrity:** a famous person

UNDERSTANDING THE READING

SUMMARIZING **A** Circle the correct words to complete the statement about priming.

Priming is a technique that [1] **advertisers / psychologists** use to persuade us to make
[2] **careful / quick** buying decisions.

IDENTIFYING
MAIN IDEAS **B** Read the sentences below. Check (✓) three that are main ideas of the passage.

☐ 1. People tend to buy more when they shop alone.

☐ 2. Priming is one way advertisers can influence people's decision-making.

☐ 3. Colors in ads can affect people's decisions to buy something.

☐ 4. Ads with photos are more likely to get people's attention.

☐ 5. The words and sounds that are used in ads can influence people's attitudes.

IDENTIFYING
SUPPORTING IDEAS **C** Match the number of each main idea in exercise B to its supporting idea.

_____ a. People are more likely to buy something because of a rhyming ad.

_____ b. It makes people decide to buy something more quickly.

_____ c. Red and green often create good feelings in people.

UNDERSTANDING
DETAILS **D** Match the priming strategies to their effects on customers.

Strategies: When ads …

_____ 1. use red

_____ 2. use green

_____ 3. limit the number we can buy

_____ 4. use rhymes

_____ 5. use celebrity power

Effects: We …

a. remember the product better

b. feel like we need to buy more

c. think a product is healthy

d. feel good about a product

e. think the product must be good
because a famous person likes it

CRITICAL THINKING:
REFLECTING **E** Look back at your answer to the question on page 71 about an interesting ad that
you noticed (exercise B-1). What techniques did the ad use? Why did it influence you?
Discuss with a partner.

Technique(s): _____

_____

Why it influenced you:

_____

_____

UNIT REVIEW

Answer the following questions.

1. What is one way advertisers persuade customers to buy their product?

   _____

   _____

   _____

2. How could you use this unit's reading skill outside of class?

   _____

   _____

   _____

3. Do you remember the meanings of these words? Check (✓) the ones you know. Look back at the unit and review the ones you don't know.

   Reading 1:

   ☐ attractive   ☐ avoid   ☐ cash

   ☐ control   ☐ instead of   ☐ percent **AWL**

   ☐ product   ☐ store   ☐ strategy **AWL**

   ☐ trust

   Reading 2:

   ☐ attitude **AWL**   ☐ customer   ☐ influence

   ☐ limit   ☐ message   ☐ natural

   ☐ notice   ☐ probably

WORD FORMS Words as Nouns and Verbs

Some words can be both nouns and verbs. Some examples are *offer*, *pick*, and *taste*. If a word follows an adjective, it is more likely to be a noun.

*I love the sweet **taste** of apples. They **taste** so fresh.*
         NOUN   VERB

A Read the sentences below. Label each underlined word as N for *noun* or V for *verb*.

1. A good meal <u>starts</u> with a great recipe.

2. It is okay to use frozen vegetables, but fresh <u>produce</u> is better.

3. In the summertime, it's fun to <u>cook</u> chicken or steaks on an outdoor <u>grill</u>.

4. He usually <u>times</u> his meals perfectly. Everything is ready before guests arrive.

5. This fresh bread <u>tastes</u> great, and the <u>smell</u> is amazing.

6. Everyone thought the dessert was a nice <u>treat</u>.

WORD FORMS Changing Adjectives into Adverbs

	ADJECTIVE	ADVERB
Many adverbs are formed by adding -*ly* to the end of adjectives. For adjectives ending in -*le*, replace the final -*e* with -*y*. For adjectives ending in -*y*, remove the final -*y* and add -*ily*.	*quick*	*quickly*
	predictable	*predictably*
	easy	*easily*

B Circle the correct words to complete the paragraph below.

Gingered Pineapple Ice Cream Sundae with Toasted Coconut

This wonderful treat was one of the most popular recipes in Sasha Martin's family. It is [1] **popular / popularly** in Sub-Saharan Africa and can be made [2] **easy / easily** with a few [3] **simple / simply** ingredients.

First, [4] **careful / carefully** cut a pineapple into small pieces and cook with ginger and brown sugar for 10 minutes. Then, pour the hot pineapple sauce over two [5] **large / largely** spoons of vanilla ice cream. [6] **Quick / Quickly** add some coconut flakes on top. The sundae is ready to eat!

VOCABULARY EXTENSION   UNIT 3

Below are definitions for common expressions with the word *living*.

standard of living: the level of wealth someone has

cost of living: the average cost of the basic necessities of life

living the dream: experiencing the achievement of all your career or life goals

make a living: to earn enough money from a job to pay for housing, food, etc.

do (something) for a living: to have a job or career

A Complete each sentence using an expression from the box above.

1. It is hard to _____ as a waiter because wages are often quite low.

2. The well-educated generally enjoy a high _____.

3. The _____ in cities like San Francisco and New York is higher than in rural areas. One of the reasons is that housing is so expensive.

4. She has the job she has always wanted—she is _____!

5. He just finished college but is not sure yet what he wants to _____.

WORD FORMS Words as Nouns and Verbs

Some words can be both nouns and verbs. Some examples are *offer*, *pick*, and *taste*. If a word follows an adjective, it is more likely to be a noun.

NOUN
*She is the most hardworking **volunteer** at the hospital.*

VERB
*She **volunteers** at the local hospital every week.*

B Read the sentences below. Write **N** for *noun* or **V** for *verb* above each underlined word.

1. Many young adults get financial <u>support</u> from their parents when buying their first house.

2. Many homeless shelters need <u>volunteers</u> to help in the kitchen.

3. After three interviews, the company <u>offered</u> me the job.

4. People tend to be happier when they have easy <u>access</u> to good, affordable healthcare.

5. The supermarket <u>rewards</u> customers who shop regularly in the store by giving them a discount.

VOCABULARY EXTENSION   UNIT 4

Some collocations are in the verb + noun form. Below are definitions of common collocations with the noun *control*.

take control: to have power or authority over something

lose control: not have power or authority over something

give (someone) control: to allow someone else to have power or authority

get (something) under control: to manage a situation better

get out of control: not manage a situation properly

A Circle the correct phrase to complete each sentence.

1. After my father retired, I became president and **took control** / **lost control** of the family business.

2. Drivers were unhappy because gas prices **got under control** / **got out of control**. Prices rose over 50 percent in just one month.

3. Online testing software **gives teachers control** / **gets teachers under control** over when and where they can give their students tests.

4. My laptop stopped working in the middle of my presentation. I was surprised but managed to **get out of control** / **get things under control**.

5. The man **gave control** / **lost control** of his car and crashed into a tree. The car was damaged but he was okay.

Some collocations are in the adjective + noun form. Below are definitions of common collocations with the adjective *natural*.

natural reaction: normal human behavior

natural food: food that has no artificial ingredients added

natural disaster: an extreme event such as an earthquake or a hurricane

natural resources: useful raw materials such as minerals, trees, oil, and water

natural history: the study of animals, plants, and natural objects

B Complete each sentence with the words below.

> disasters   foods   history   reaction   resources

1. Hurricane Katrina was one of the worst natural _____ to hit the United States.

2. Many natural _____ museums have dinosaur fossils.

3. It is a natural _____ to laugh when someone tickles you.

4. Conservationists think we should protect and preserve our natural _____ for future generations.

5. Supermarkets have seen increasing demand for natural _____ in recent years.

GRAMMAR REFERENCE

UNIT 1
Language for Writing: Giving Reasons

Use the transition word *because* to show a reason.

Notes	Examples
Because is a conjunction. It connects ideas between sentences. It shows a reason.	REASON Adam Roberts started a food blog **because** he needed a break.
Because introduces a dependent clause. A dependent clause must have a subject and a verb.	DEPENDENT CLAUSE Roberts started a food blog because **he needed** a break. SUBJECT VERB
The dependent clause with *because* can start a sentence. Add a comma to separate the clauses.	**Because** he needed a break from school, Roberts started a food blog.

Use *in order* to show a reason.

Notes	Examples
Use *in order* with an infinitive to show a reason.	REASON Some people start blogs **in order** to tell their friends about their daily lives.
The infinitive can be used without *in order*.	Some people start blogs **to tell** their friends about their daily lives.

UNIT 3
Language for Writing: Review of the Simple Present Tense

Affirmative and Negative Statements with *Be*					
Affirmative Statements			**Negative Statements**		
Subject	*Am/Are/Is*		Subject	*Am/Are/Is Not*	
I	**am**	happy. busy. online. at home.	I	**am not**	happy. busy. online. at home.
You We They	**are**		You We They	**are not** **aren't**	
He She It	**is**		He She It	**is not** **isn't**	

Affirmative and Negative Statements: Other Verbs				
Affirmative Statements		**Negative Statements**		
Subject	Verb	Subject	*Do/Does Not*	Verb (Base Form)
I You We They	**live** in Singapore.	I You We They	**do not** **don't**	**live** in Mexico.
He She It	**lives** in Singapore.	He She It	**does not** **doesn't**	

UNIT 4
Language for Writing: Connecting Ideas

The words and phrases below help connect ideas between sentences.

Notes	Examples
Use *in addition, furthermore*, and *also* to give additional information about an idea.	Advertisers know that consumers like watching their favorite celebrities. **Furthermore**, consumers are willing to buy products featuring celebrities.
Add a comma after the transition word or phrase that comes at the beginning of a sentence.	**In addition**, celebrities can help reach a larger number of people.
Some transition words or phrases can be put before the main verb. Add commas before and after the transition word or phrase.	Celebrities can, **in addition**, help reach a larger number of people.
Also does not usually need commas when used.	Celebrities can **also** help reach a larger number of people.

EDITING CHECKLIST

Use the checklist to find errors in your writing task for each unit.

	WRITING TASK	
	1	2
1. Is the first word of every sentence capitalized?		
2. Does every sentence end with the correct punctuation?		
3. Do your subjects and verbs agree?		
4. Are commas used in the right places?		
5. Do all possessive nouns have an apostrophe?		
6. Are all proper nouns capitalized?		
7. Is the spelling of places, people, and other proper nouns correct?		
8. Did you check for frequently confused words?		

Brief Writer's Handbook

Understanding the Writing Process: The Seven Steps

The Assignment

Imagine that you have been given the following assignment: *Write a definition paragraph about an everyday item.*

What should you do first? What should you do second, third, and so on? There are many ways to write, but most good writers follow certain general steps in the writing process.

Look at this list of steps. Which ones do you usually do? Which ones have you never done?

STEP 1: Choose a topic.

STEP 2: Brainstorm.

STEP 3: Outline.

STEP 4: Write the first draft.

STEP 5: Get feedback from a peer.

STEP 6: Revise the first draft.

STEP 7: Proofread the final draft.

Now you will see how one student went through all the steps to do the assignment. First, read the final paragraph that Susan gave her teacher. Read the teacher's comments as well.

Example Paragraph 1

Gumbo

The dictionary definition of *gumbo* does not make gumbo sound as delicious as it really is. The dictionary defines gumbo as a "thick soup made in south Louisiana." However, anyone who has tasted this delicious dish knows that this definition is too bland to describe gumbo. It is true that gumbo is a thick soup, but it is much more than that. Gumbo, one of the most popular of all Cajun dishes, is made with different kinds of seafood or meat mixed with vegetables, such as green peppers and onions. For example, seafood gumbo contains shrimp and crab. Other kinds of gumbo include chicken, sausage, or turkey. Regardless of the ingredients in gumbo, this regional delicacy is very delicious.

Teacher comments:

100/A⁺   Excellent paragraph!
  I enjoyed reading about gumbo. Your paragraph is very well written. All the sentences relate to one single topic. I really like the fact that you used so many connectors—however, such as.

Now look at the steps that Susan went through to compose the paragraph that you just read.

Steps in the Writing Process
Step 1: Choose a Topic
Susan chose gumbo as her topic. This is what she wrote about her choice.

When I first saw the assignment, I did not know what to write about. I did not think I was going to be able to find a good topic.

First, I tried to think of something that I could define. It could not be something that was really simple like television or a car. Everyone already knows what they are. I thought that I should choose something that most people might not know.

I tried to think of general areas like sports, machines, and inventions. However, I chose food as my general area. Everyone likes food.

Then I had to find one kind of food that not everyone knows. For me, that was not too difficult. My family is from Louisiana, and the food in Louisiana is special. It is not the usual food that most Americans eat. One of the dishes we eat a lot in Louisiana is gumbo, which is a kind of thick soup. I thought gumbo would be a good topic for a definition paragraph because not many people know it, and it is sort of easy for me to write a definition for this food.

Another reason that gumbo is a good choice for a definition paragraph is that I know a lot about this kind of food. I know how to make it, I know what the ingredients are, and I know what it tastes like. It is much easier to write about something that I know than about something that I do not know about.

After I was sure that gumbo was going to be my topic, I went on to the next step, which is brainstorming.

Susan's notes about choosing her topic

Step 2: Brainstorm

The next step for Susan was to brainstorm ideas about her topic.

In this step, you write down every idea that pops into your head about your topic. Some of these ideas will be good, and some will be bad—write them all down. The main purpose of brainstorming is to write down as many ideas as you can think of. If one idea looks especially good, you might circle that idea or put a check mark next to it. If you write down an idea and you know right away that you are not going to use it, you can cross it out.

Look at Susan's brainstorming diagram on the topic of gumbo.

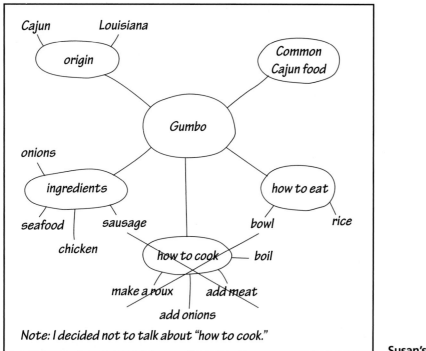

Susan's brainstorming diagram

Step 3: Outline

At this point, some writers want to start writing, but that is not the best plan. After you brainstorm your ideas, the next step is to make an outline. An outline helps you organize how you will present your information. It helps you see which areas of the paragraph are strong and which are weak.

After brainstorming, Susan studied her list of ideas. She then made a simple outline of what her paragraph might look like. Some writers prepare very detailed outlines, but many writers just make a list of the main points and some of the details for each main point.

Read the outline that Susan wrote.

> What is gumbo?
> 1. A simple definition of gumbo.
> 2. A longer definition of gumbo.
> 3. A list of the different ingredients of gumbo.
>   A. seafood or meat
>   B. with vegetables (onions)
>   C. seafood gumbo
> 4. How gumbo is served.

Susan's outline

As you can see, this outline is very basic. There are also some problems. For example, Susan repeats some items in different parts of the outline. In addition, she does not have a concluding sentence. These errors will probably be corrected at the first draft step, the peer editing step, or the final draft step.

Step 4: Write the First Draft

Next, Susan wrote a first draft. In this step, you use the information from your outline and from your brainstorming session to write a first draft. This first draft may contain many errors, such as misspellings, incomplete ideas, and incorrect punctuation. At this point, do not worry about correcting the errors. The main goal is to put your ideas into sentences.

You may feel that you do not know what you think about the topic yet. In this case, it may be difficult for you to write, but it is important to start the process of writing. Sometimes writing helps you think, and as soon as you form a new thought, you can write it down.

Read Susan's first draft, including her notes to herself.

Introduction is weak ??? Use dictionary!

(Rough draft)
Susan Mims

○ Do you know what gumbo is. It's a seafood soup. However, gumbo is really more than a kind of soup, it's special. ???

Gumbo is one of the most popular of all Cajun dish. es

Combine {
It's made with various kind of seafood or meet. meat
This is mixed with vegetables such as onions. green peppers
}

Combine {
Seafood gumbo is made with shrimp and crab.
Also chicken, sausage, and turkey, etc. Regardless ok???
of what is in gumbo, it's usually served in bowl
over the rice. — Is this correct? Ask teacher!
}

○

Susan's first draft

What do you notice about this first draft? Here are a few things that a good writer should pay attention to:

- First of all, remember that this paper is not the final draft. Even native speakers who are good writers usually write more than one draft. You will have a chance to revise the paper and make it better.

- Look at the circles, question marks, and writing in the margin. These are notes that Susan made to herself about what to change, add, or reconsider.

- Remember that the paper will go through the peer-editing process later. Another reader will help you make your meaning clear and will look for errors.

In addition to the language errors that writers often make in the first draft, the handwriting is usually not neat. Sometimes it is so messy that only the writer can read it!

Step 5: Get Feedback from a Peer

Peer editing a draft is a critical step toward the final goal of excellent writing. Sometimes it is difficult for writers to see the weaknesses in their own writing, so receiving advice from another writer can be very helpful.

Ask a colleague, friend, or classmate to read your writing and to offer suggestions about how to improve it. Some people do not like criticism, but constructive criticism is always helpful for writers. Remember that even professional writers have editors, so do not be embarrassed to receive help.

Susan exchanged papers with another student, Jim, in her class. On the next page is the peer editing sheet that Jim completed about Susan's paragraph. Read the questions and answers.

Peer Editing Sheet

Writer: _Susan_   Date: _2-14_

Peer Editor: _Jim_

1. What is the general topic of the paper? _gumbo_

2. What is the writer's purpose? (in 15 words or less)
   to define gumbo

3. Is the paragraph indented? ☑ yes ☐ no

4. How many sentences are there? _6_

5. Is the first word of every sentence capitalized? ☑ yes ☐ no
   If you answered *no,* circle the problem(s) on the paper.

6. Does every sentence end with correct punctuation? ☐ yes ☑ no
   If you answered *no,* circle the problem(s) on the paper.

7. Are there any other capitalization or punctuation errors? ☑ yes ☐ no
   If you answered *yes,* circle the problem(s) on the paper.

8. Write the topic sentence here.
   You have two sentences: Do you know what gumbo is. It is a seafood soup.

9. Do you think the topic sentence is good for this paragraph? Comments?
   No, you need one sentence that introduces your topic and purpose better.

10. Does the paragraph talk about just one topic? ☑ yes ☐ no

    If you answered *no,* what is the extra topic? _____

    In what sentence is this extra topic introduced? _____

11. Does every sentence have a verb? ❑ yes ☑ no

If you answered *no,* circle the error(s)on the paper.

12. Write any mistakes that you found. Add appropriate corrections.

Error 1: _it's-don't use contractions in formal writing_____

Correction: _it is_____

Error 2: _etc.-don't use this_____

Correction: _You should list all the kinds._____

Error 3: _____

Correction: _____

13. Did you have any trouble understanding this paragraph? ❑ yes ☑ no

If you answered *yes,* tell where and/or why.

_____

14. What questions do you have about the content? What other information should be in this paragraph?

How do you make gumbo? Is it easy to cook? Why do you think people started making gumbo?

15. What is your opinion of the writing of this paragraph?

It is good, but the concluding sentence gives new information. It does not conclude! Also,

do not repeat the word "gumbo" so much. Do not use "is" so much! Use other verbs.

16. What is your opinion of the content of this paragraph?

I like the topic. I think I ate gumbo at a restaurant once.

Step 6: Revise the First Draft

In this step, you will see how Susan used the suggestions and information to revise her paragraph. This step consists of three parts:

1. React to the comments on the peer editing sheet.

2. Reread the paragraph and make changes.

3. Rewrite the paragraph one more time.

Here is what Susan wrote about the changes she decided to make.

> I read my paragraph again several times. Each time I read it, I found things that I wanted to change in some way. Sometimes I corrected an obvious error. Other times I added words to make my writing clear to the reader. Based on Jim's suggestion, I used "this delicious dish" and other expressions instead of repeating "gumbo" so many times.
>
> I used some of Jim's suggestions, but I did not use all of them. I thought that some of his questions were interesting, but the answers were not really part of the purpose of this paragraph, which was to define gumbo.
>
> I was happy that the peer editor was able to understand all my ideas fully. To me, this means that my writing is good enough.

Susan's notes about changes she decided to make

Step 7: Proofread the Final Draft

Most of the hard work should be over by now. In this step, the writer pretends to be a brand-new reader who has never seen the paper before. The writer reads the paper to see if the sentences and ideas flow smoothly.

Read Susan's final paper again on page 83. Notice any changes in vocabulary, grammar, spelling, or punctuation that she made at this stage.

Of course, the very last step is to turn the paper in to your teacher and hope that you get a good grade!

Editing Your Writing

While you must be comfortable writing quickly, you also need to be comfortable with improving your work. Writing an assignment is never a one-step process. For even the most gifted writers, it is often a multiple-step process. When you were completing your assignments in this book, you probably made some changes to your work to make it better. However, you may not have fixed all of the errors. The paper that you turned in to your teacher is called a **first draft,** which is sometimes referred to as a **rough draft.**

A first draft can almost always be improved. One way to improve your writing is to ask a classmate, friend, or teacher to read it and make suggestions. Your reader may discover that one of your paragraphs is missing a topic sentence, that you have made grammar mistakes, or that your essay needs different vocabulary choices. You may not always like or agree with the comments from a reader, but being open to changes will make you a better writer.

This section will help you become more familiar with how to identify and correct errors in your writing.

Step 1

Below is a student's first draft for a timed writing. The writing prompt for this assignment, was "Many schools now offer classes online. Which do you prefer and why?" As you read the first draft, look for areas that need improvement and write your comments. For example, does every sentence have a subject and a verb? Does the writer always use the correct verb tense and punctuation? Does the paragraph have a topic sentence with controlling ideas? Is the vocabulary suitable for the intended audience? What do you think of the content?

The Online Courses

Online courses are very popular at my university. I prefered traditional face-to-face classes. At my university, students have a choice between courses that are taught online in a virtual classroom and the regular kind of classroom. I know that many students prefer online classes, but I cannot adjust to that style of educate. For me, is important to have a professor who explains the material to everyone "live" and then answer any questions that we have. Sometimes students might think they understand the material until the professor questions, and then we realize that we did not understand everything. At that moment, the professor then offers other explanation to help bridge the gap. I do not see this kind of spontaneous learning and teaching can take place online. I have never taken an online course until now. Some of my friends like online courses because they can take the class at his own convenience instead of have to assist class at a set time. However, these supposed conveniences are not outweigh the educational advantages that traditional face-to-face classes offer.

Step 2

Read the teacher comments on the first draft of "The Online Courses." Are these the same things that you noticed?

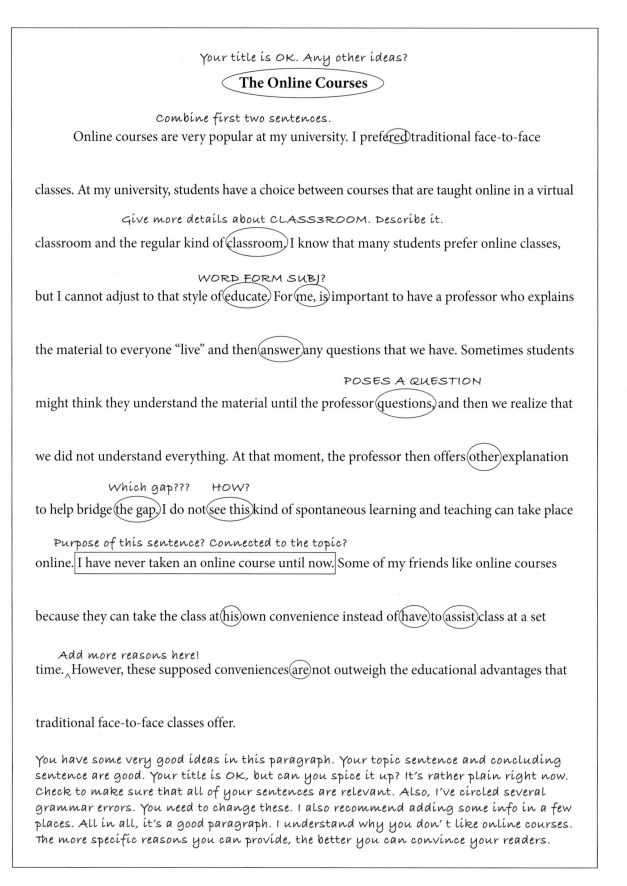

Your title is OK. Any other ideas?

The Online Courses

Combine first two sentences.

Online courses are very popular at my university. I prefered traditional face-to-face

classes. At my university, students have a choice between courses that are taught online in a virtual

Give more details about CLASS3ROOM. Describe it.

classroom and the regular kind of classroom. I know that many students prefer online classes,

WORD FORM SUBJ?

but I cannot adjust to that style of educate. For me, is important to have a professor who explains

the material to everyone "live" and then answer any questions that we have. Sometimes students

POSES A QUESTION

might think they understand the material until the professor questions, and then we realize that

we did not understand everything. At that moment, the professor then offers other explanation

Which gap???   HOW?

to help bridge the gap. I do not see this kind of spontaneous learning and teaching can take place

Purpose of this sentence? Connected to the topic?

online. I have never taken an online course until now. Some of my friends like online courses

because they can take the class at his own convenience instead of have to assist class at a set

Add more reasons here!

time. However, these supposed conveniences are not outweigh the educational advantages that

traditional face-to-face classes offer.

You have some very good ideas in this paragraph. Your topic sentence and concluding
sentence are good. Your title is OK, but can you spice it up? It's rather plain right now.
Check to make sure that all of your sentences are relevant. Also, I've circled several
grammar errors. You need to change these. I also recommend adding some info in a few
places. All in all, it's a good paragraph. I understand why you don't like online courses.
The more specific reasons you can provide, the better you can convince your readers.

Step 3

Now read the writer's second draft of the paragraph. How is it the same as the first draft? How is it different? Did the writer fix all the sentence mistakes?

Online Courses

Online courses are very popular at my university but I prefer traditional face-to-face classes. At my university students have a choice between courses that are taught online in a virtual classroom and the regular kind of classroom with a room, a professor, and students in chairs. I know that many students prefer online classes, but I cannot adjust to that style of education. For me, it is important to have a professor who explains the material to everyone "live" and then answers any questions that we might have. Sometimes students might think they understand the material until the professor poses a question, and then we realize that we did not understand everything. At that moment, the professor then offers another explanation to help bridge the gap between our knowledge and the truth. I do not see how this kind of spontaneous leaerning and teaching can take place online. Some of my friends like online courses because they can take the class at their own convenience instead of having to attend class at a set time. They also like to save transportation money and time. However, these supposed conveniences do not outweigh the many educational advantages that traditional face-to-face classes offer.

Capitalization Activities
Basic Capitalization Rules

1. Always capitalize the first word of a sentence.

   Today is not Sunday.

   It is not Saturday either.

   Do you know today's date?

2. Always capitalize the word *I* no matter where it is in a sentence.

   John brought the dessert, and I brought some drinks.

   I want some tea.

   The winners of the contest were Ned and I.

3. Capitalize proper nouns—the names of specific people, places, or things. Capitalize a person's title, including Mr., Mrs., Ms., and Dr. Compare these example pairs.

   Proper nouns: When our teacher Mr. Hill visited his home state of Arizona, he took a short trip to see the Grand Canyon.

   Common nouns: When our teacher visited his home state, he saw many mountains and canyons.

   Proper nouns: The Statue of Liberty is located on Liberty Island in New York.

   Common nouns: There is a famous statue on that island, isn't there?

4. Capitalize names of countries and other geographic areas. Capitalize the names of people from those areas. Capitalize the names of languages.

   People from Brazil are called Brazilians. They speak Portuguese.

   People from Germany are called Germans. They speak German.

5. Capitalize titles of works, such as books, movies, and pieces of art. If you look at the example paragraphs in this book, you will notice that each of them begins with a title. In a title, pay attention to which words begin with a capital letter and which words do not.

Gumbo	*A Lesson in Friendship*	*An Immigrant in the Family*
The King and I	*The Tale of Pinocchio*	*Love at First Sight*

   The rules for capitalizing titles are easy.

   - Always capitalize the first letter of a title.

   - If the title has more than one word, capitalize all the words that have meaning (content words).

   - Do not capitalize small (function) words, such as *a, an, and, the, in, with, on, for, to, above,* and *or.*

Capitalization Activities

ACTIVITY 1

Circle the words that have capitalization errors. Make the corrections above the errors.

1. the last day to sign up for the trip to sao paolo is this Thursday.

2. does jill live in west bay apartments, too?

3. the flight to Vancouver left late Saturday night and arrived early Sunday morning.

4. My sister has two daughters. Their names are rachel and rosalyn.

5. one of the most important sporting events is the world cup.

ACTIVITY 2

Complete these statements. Be sure to use correct capitalization.

1. *U.S.A.* stands for the United _____ of _____ .

2. The seventh month of the year is _____ .

3. _____ is the capital of Brazil.

4. One of the most popular brands of jeans is _____ .

5. The first person to walk on the moon was named _____ .

6. Parts of Europe were destroyed in _____ (1914–18).

7. My favorite restaurant is _____ .

8. Beijing is the largest city in _____ .

9. The winter months are _____ , _____ , and _____ .

10. The last movie that I saw was _____ .

ACTIVITY 3

Read the following titles. Rewrite them with correct capitalization.

1. my favorite food _____

2. living in montreal _____

3. the best restaurant in town _____

4. my best friend's new car _____

5. a new trend in Hollywood _____

6. why i left my country _____

7. my side of the mountain _____

8. no more room for a friend _____

Read the following paragraph. Circle the capitalization errors and make corrections above the errors.

Example Paragraph 2

A visit to Cuba

according to an article in last week's issue of *time*, the prime minister of canada will visit cuba soon in order to establish better economic ties between the two countries. because the united states does not have a history of good relations with cuba, canada's recent decision may result in problems between washington and ottawa. In an interview, the canadian prime minister indicated that his country was ready to reestablish some sort of cooperation with cuba and that canada would do so as quickly as possible. there is no doubt that this new development will be discussed at the opening session of congress next tuesday.

ACTIVITY 5

Read the following paragraph. Circle the capitalization errors and make corrections above the errors.

Example Paragraph 3

crossing the atlantic from atlanta

it used to be difficult to travel directly from atlanta to europe, but this is certainly not the case nowadays. union airways offers several daily flights to london. jetwings express offers flights every day to frankfurt and twice a week to berlin. other european air carriers that offer direct flights from atlanta to europe are valuair and luxliner. However, the airline with the largest number of direct flights to any european city is not a european airline. smead airlines, which is a new and rising airline in the united states, offers 17 flights a day to 12 european cities, including paris, london, frankfurt, zurich, rome, and athens.

Read the following paragraph. Circle the capitalization errors and make corrections above the errors.

my beginnings in foreign languages

I have always loved foreign languages. When I was in tenth grade, I took my first foreign language class. It was french I. My teacher was named mrs. montluzin. She was a wonderful teacher who inspired me to develop my interest in foreign languages. Before I finished high school, I took a second year of french and one year of spanish. I wish my high school had offered latin or greek, but the small size of the school body prevented this. Over the years since I graduated from high school, I have lived and worked abroad. I studied arabic when I lived in saudi arabia, japanese in japan, and malay in malaysia. Two years ago, I took a german class in the united states. Because of recent travels to uzbekistan and kyrgyzstan, which are two republics from the former soviet union, I have a strong desire to study russian. I hope that my love of learning foreign languages will continue.

Punctuation Activities
End Punctuation

The three most common punctuation marks found at the end of English sentences are the **period**, the **question mark**, and the **exclamation point**. It is important to know how to use all three of them correctly. Of these three, however, the period is by far the most commonly used punctuation mark.

1. **period** (.) A period is used at the end of a declarative sentence.

   This sentence is a declarative sentence.

   This sentence is not a question.

   All three of these sentences end with a period.

2. **question mark** (?) A question mark is used at the end of a question.

   Is this idea difficult?

   Is it hard to remember the name of this mark?

   How many questions are in this group?

3. **exclamation point** (!) An exclamation point is used at the end of an exclamation. It is less common than the other two marks.

> I cannot believe you think this topic is difficult**!**

> This is the best writing book in the world**!**

> Now I understand all of these examples**!**

ACTIVITY 1

Add the correct end punctuation.

1. Congratulations

2. Do most people think that the governor was unaware of the theft

3. Do not open your test booklet until you are told to do so

4. Will the president attend the meeting

5. Jason put the dishes in the dishwasher and then watched TV

ACTIVITY 2

Look at an article in any English newspaper or magazine. Circle every end punctuation mark. Then answer these questions.

1. How many final periods are there? _____ (or _____ %)

2. How many final question marks are there? _____ (or _____ %)

3. How many final exclamation points are there? _____ (or _____ %)

4. What is the total number of sentences? _____

Use this last number to calculate the percentages for each of the categories. Does the period occur most often?

Commas

The comma has several different functions in English. Here are some of the most common ones.

1. A comma separates a list of three or more things. There should be a comma between the items in a list.

> He speaks French and English. (No comma is needed because there are only two items.)

> She speaks French**,** English**,** and Chinese.

2. A comma separates two sentences when there is a combining word (coordinating conjunction) such as *and, but, or, so, for, nor,* and *yet.* The easy way to remember these conjunctions is *FANBOYS (for, and, nor, but, or, yet, so).*

> Six people took the course**,** but only five of them passed the test.

> Sammy bought the cake**,** and Paul paid for the ice cream.

> Students can register for classes in person**,** or they may submit their applications by mail.

3. A comma is used to separate an introductory word or phrase from the rest of the sentence.

> In conclusion**,** doctors are advising people to take more vitamins.

> First**,** you will need a pencil.

> Because of the heavy rains**,** many of the roads were flooded.

> Finally**,** add the nuts to the batter.

4. A comma is used to separate an appositive from the rest of the sentence. An appositive is a word or group of words that renames a noun before it. An appositive provides additional information about the noun.

subject (noun)   appositive   verb

Washington, the first president of the United States, was a clever military leader.

In this sentence, the phrase *the first president of the United States* is an appositive. This phrase renames or explains the noun *Washington*.

5. A comma is sometimes used with adjective clauses. An adjective clause usually begins with a relative pronoun *(who, that, which, whom, whose, whoever,* or *whomever).* We use a comma when the information in the clause is unnecessary or extra. (This is also called a nonrestrictive clause.)

The book <u>that is on the teacher's desk</u> is the main book for this class.

(Here, when you say "the book," the reader does not know which book you are talking about, so the information in the adjective clause is necessary. In this case, do not set off the adjective clause with a comma.)

The History of Korea, <u>which is on the teacher's desk,</u> is the main book for this class.

(The name of the book is given, so the information in the adjective clause is not necessary to help the reader identify the book. In this case, you must use commas to show that the information in the adjective clause is extra, or nonrestrictive.)

ACTIVITY 3

Add commas as needed in these sentences. Some sentences may be correct, and others may need more than one comma.

1. For the past fifteen years Mary Parker has been both the director and producer of all the plays at this theater.

2. Despite all the problems we had on our vacation we managed to have a good time.

3. I believe the best countries to visit in Africa are Senegal Tunisia and Ghana.

4. She believes the best countries to visit in Africa are Senegal and Tunisia.

5. The third step in this process is to grate the carrots and the potatoes.

6. Third grate the carrots and the potatoes.

7. Blue green and red are strong colors. For this reason they are not appropriate for a living room wall.

8. Without anyone to teach foreign language classes next year the school will be unable to offer French Spanish or German.

9. The NEQ 7000 the very latest computer from Electron Technologies is not selling very well.

10. Because of injuries neither Carl nor Jamil two of the best players on the football team will be able to play in tomorrow's game.

11. The job interview is for a position at Mills Trust Company which is the largest company in this area.

12. The job interview is for a position at a large company that has more than 1,000 employees in this area.

13. Kevin's birthday is January 18 which is the same day that Laura and Greg have their birthdays.

14. Martina Navratilova whom most tennis fans refer to only as Martina dominated women's tennis for years.

15. My brother who lives in San Salvador has two children. (I have several brothers.)

16. My brother who lives in San Salvador has two children. (I have only one brother.)

17. This flight is leaving for La Paz which is the first of three stops that the plane will make.

18. No one knows the name of the person who will take over the committee in January so there have been many rumors about this.

19. Greenfield Central Bank the most recent bank to open a branch here in our area has tried to establish a branch here for years.

20. On the right side of the living room an antique radio sits on top of a glass table that also has a flowerpot a photo of a baby and a magazine.

Apostrophes

Apostrophes have two basic uses in English. They indicate either a contraction or possession.

Contractions: Use an apostrophe in a contraction in place of the letter or letters that have been deleted.

> He's (he is *or* he has), they're (they are), I've (I have), we'd (we would *or* we had)

Possession: Use an apostrophe to indicate possession. Add an apostrophe and the letter *s* after the word. If a plural word already ends in *s*, then just add an apostrophe.

> Gandhi's role in the history of India
> Yesterday's paper
> the boy's books (One boy has some books.)
> the boys' books (Several boys have one or more books.)

ACTIVITY 4

Correct the apostrophe errors in these sentences.

1. I am going to Victors birthday party on Saturday.

2. My three cousins house is right next to Mr. Wilsons house.

3. Hardly anyone remembers Stalins drastic actions in the early part of the last century.

4. It goes without saying that wed be better off without so much poverty in this world.

5. The reasons that were given for the childrens bad behavior were unbelievable.

Quotation Marks

Below are three of the most common uses for quotation marks.

1. To mark the exact words that were spoken by someone:

   The king said, "I refuse to give up my throne." (The period is inside the quotation marks.)*

   "None of the solutions is correct," said the professor. (The comma is inside the quotation marks.)*

   The king said that he refuses to give up his throne. (No quotation marks are needed because the sentence does not include the king's exact words. This style is called indirect speech.)

   * Note that the comma separates the verb that tells the form of communications (*said, announced, wrote*) and the quotation.

2. To mark language that a writer has borrowed from another source:

   The dictionary defines gossip as an "informal conversation, often about other people's private affairs," but I would add that it is usually malicious.

   This research concludes that there was "no real reason to expect this computer software program to produce good results with high school students."

   According to an article in *The San Jose Times,* about half of the money was stolen. (No quotes are necessary here because it is a summary of information rather than exact words from the article.)

3. To indicate when a word or phrase is being used in a special way:

   The king believed himself to be the leader of a democracy, so he allowed the prisoner to choose his method of dying. According to the king, allowing this kind of "democracy" showed that he was indeed a good ruler.

ACTIVITY 5

Add quotation marks where necessary. Remember the rules for placing commas, periods, and question marks inside or outside the quotation marks.

1. As I was leaving the room, I heard the teacher say, Be sure to study Chapter 7.

2. It is impossible to say that using dictionaries is useless. However, according to research published in the latest issue of the *General Language Journal,* dictionary use is down. I found the article's statement that 18.3 percent of students do not own a dictionary and 37.2 percent never use their dictionary (p. 75) to be rather shocking.

   Source: Wendt, John "Dictionary Use by Language Students," *General Language Journal* 3 (2007): 72-101.

3. My fiancée says that if I buy her a huge diamond ring, this would be a sign that I love her. I would like to know if there is a less expensive sign that would be a sure sign of my love for her.

4. When my English friend speaks of a heat wave just because the temperature reaches over 80°, I have to laugh because I come from Thailand, where we have sunshine most of the year. The days when we have to dress warmly are certainly few, and some people wear shorts outside almost every month of the year.

5. The directions on the package read, Open carefully. Add contents to one glass of warm water. Drink just before bedtime.

Semicolons

The semicolon is used most often to combine two related sentences. Once you get used to using the semicolon, you will find that it is a very easy and useful punctuation tool to vary the sentences in your writing.

- Use a semicolon when you want to connect two simple sentences.

- The function of a semicolon is similar to that of a period. However, in order to use a semicolon, there must be a relationship between the sentences.

    Joey loves to play tennis. He has been playing since he was ten years old.

    Joey loves to play tennis; he has been playing since he was ten years old.

Both sentence pairs are correct. The main difference is that the semicolon in the second example signals the relationship between the ideas in the two sentences. Notice also that *he* is not capitalized in the second example.

ACTIVITY 6

The following sentences use periods for separation. Rewrite the sentences. Replace the periods with semicolons and make any other necessary changes.

1. Gretchen and Bob have been friends since elementary school. They are also next-door neighbors.

   _____

2. The test was complicated. No one passed it.

   _____

3. Tomatoes are necessary for a garden salad. Peas are not.

   _____

4. Mexico lies to the south of the United States. Canada lies to the north.

   _____

Look at a copy of an English newspaper or magazine. Circle all the semicolons on a page. The number should be relatively small.

NOTE: If the topic of the article is technical or complex, there is a greater chance of finding semicolons. Semicolons are not usually used in informal or friendly writing. Thus, you might see a semicolon in an article about heart surgery or educational research, but not in an ad for a household product or an e-mail or text message to a friend.

Editing for Errors

ACTIVITY 8

Find the 14 punctuation errors in this paragraph and make corrections above the errors.

Example Paragraph 5

An Unexpected Storm

Severe weather is a constant possibility all over the globe; but we never really expect our own area to be affected However last night was different At about ten o'clock a tornado hit Lucedale This violent weather destroyed nine homes near the downtown area In addition to these nine houses that were completely destroyed many others in the area had heavy damage Amazingly no one was injured in last nights terrible storm Because of the rapid reaction of state and local weather watchers most of the areas residents saw the warnings that were broadcast on television

ACTIVITY 9

Find the 15 punctuation errors in this paragraph and make corrections above the errors.

Example Paragraph 6

Deserts

Deserts are some of the most interesting places on earth A desert is not just a dry area it is an area that receives less than ten inches of rainfall a year About one-fifth of the earth is composed of deserts Although many people believe that deserts are nothing but hills of sand this is not true In reality deserts have large rocks mountains canyons and even lakes For instance only about ten percent of the Sahara Desert the largest desert on the earth is sand

Find the 15 punctuation errors in this paragraph and make corrections above the errors.

Example Paragraph 7

A Review

I Wish I Could Have Seen His Face Marilyn Kings latest novel
is perhaps her greatest triumph In this book King tells the story of the
Lamberts a poor family that struggles to survive despite numerous
hardships. The Lambert family consists of five strong personalities.
Michael Lambert has trouble keeping a job and Naomi earns very little
as a maid at a hotel The three children range in age from nine to sixteen.
Dan Melinda and Zeke are still in school This well-written novel allows
us to step into the conflict that each of the children has to deal with. Only
a writer as talented as King could develop five independent characters in
such an outstanding manner The plot has many unexpected turns and the
outcome of this story will not disappoint readers While King has written
several novels that won international praise *I Wish I Could Have Seen His
Face* is in many ways better than any of her previous works.

Additional Grammar Activities
Verb Tense

ACTIVITY 1

Fill in the blanks with the verb that best completes the sentence. Be sure to use the correct form of the
verb. Use the following verbs: *like, cut, break, stir,* and *spread.*

Example Paragraph 8

A Simple Sandwich

Making a tuna salad sandwich is not difficult. Put two cans of flaked
tuna in a medium-sized bowl. With a fork, _____ the fish
apart. _____ up a large white onion or two small yellow
onions. _____ in one-third cup of mayonnaise. Then

add salt and pepper to taste. Some people _____ to mix

pieces of boiled eggs into their salad. Once you finish making the salad,

_____ it between two slices of bread. Now you are ready to

eat your easy-to-make treat.

ACTIVITY 2

Fill in the blanks with the correct form of any appropriate verb.

Who Killed Kennedy?

One of the most infamous moments in U.S. history _____

in 1963. In that year, President John F. Kennedy _____

assassinated in Dallas, Texas. Since this event, there _____

many theories about what _____ on that fateful day.

According to the official U.S. government report, only one man

_____ the bullets that _____ President

Kennedy. However, even today many people _____ that

there _____ several assassins.

ACTIVITY 3

Fill in the blanks with the correct form of any appropriate verb.

A Routine Routine

I have one of the most boring daily routines of anyone I

_____ . Every morning, I _____ at 7:15.1

_____ a shower and _____ dressed.

After that, I _____ breakfast and _____

to the office. I _____ from 8:30 to 4:30. Then I

_____ home. This _____ five days a week

without fail. Just for once, I wish something different would happen!

Fill in the blanks with the correct form of the verbs in parentheses.

Example Paragraph 11

The Shortest Term in the White House

William Henry Harrison (be) _____ the ninth president of the United States. His presidency was extremely brief. In fact, Harrison (be) _____ president for only one month. He (take) _____ office on March 4,1841. Unfortunately he (catch) _____ a cold that (become) _____ pneumonia. On April 4, Harrison (die) _____ . He (become) _____ the first American president to die while in office. Before becoming president, Harrison (study) _____ to become a doctor and later (serve) _____ in the army.

ACTIVITY 5

Fill in the blanks with the correct form of the verbs in parentheses.

Example Paragraph 12

The History of Brownsville

Brownsville, Texas, is a city with an interesting history. Brownsville (be) _____ originally a fort during the Mexican-American War. During that war, American and Mexican soldiers (fight) _____ several battles in the area around the city. As a matter of fact, the city (get) _____ its name from Major Jacob Brown, an American soldier who was killed in a battle near the old fort. However, Brownsville's history (be) _____ not only connected to war. After the war, the city was best known for farming. The area's rich soil (help) _____ it become a thriving agriculture center. Over time, the agricultural industry (grow) _____ , and today Brownsville farmers (be) _____ well-known for growing cotton and citrus. In sum, both the Mexican-American War and farming have played important historical roles in making Brownsville such an interesting city.

Articles

ACTIVITY 6

Fill in the blanks with the correct article. If no article is required, write an X in the blank.

_____ Simple Math Problem

There is _____ interesting mathematics brainteaser that always amazes _____ people when they first hear it. First, pick _____ number from _____ 1 to _____ 9. Subtract _____ 5. (You may have a negative number.) Multiply this answer by _____ 3. Now square _____ number. Then add _____ digits of _____ number. For _____ example, if your number is 81, add 8 and 1 to get an answer of _____ 9. If _____ number is less than _____ 5, add _____ 5. If _____ number is not less than _____ 5, subtract _____ 4. Now multiply this number by _____ 2. Finally, subtract _____ 6. If you have followed _____ steps correctly, _____ your answer is _____ 4.

ACTIVITY 7

Fill in the blanks with the correct article. If no article is required, write an X in the blank.

_____ Geography Problems among _____ American Students

Are _____ American high school students _____ less educated in _____ geography than high school students in _____ other countries? According to _____ recent survey of _____ high school students all over _____ globe, _____ U.S. students do not know very much about _____ geography. For _____

example, _____ surprisingly large number did not know

_____ capital of _____ state in which

they live. Many could not find _____ Mexico on a map

even though Mexico is one of _____ two countries

that share _____ border with _____

United States. Some _____ educators blame this lack of

_____ geographical knowledge on the move away from

memorization of material that has taken _____ place

in _____ recent years in American schools. Regardless

of _____ cause, the unfortunate fact appears to be that

American _____ high school students are not learning

enough about this subject area.

ACTIVITY 8

Fill in the blanks with the correct article. If no article is required, write an X in the blank.

Example Paragraph 15

_____ **Homeowners Saving** _____ **Money with a New Free Service**

People who are concerned that their monthly electricity

bill is too high can now take _____ advantage of

_____ special free service offered by the local electricity

company. _____ company will do _____

home energy audit on any house to find out if _____

house is wasting _____ valuable energy. Homeowners

can call _____ power company to schedule _____

convenient time for _____ energy analyst to visit

their home. The audit takes only about _____ hour.

_____ analyst will inspect _____

home and identify potential energy-saving _____

improvements. For _____ example, he or she will

check _____ thermostat, the air-conditioning, and

_____ seals around doors and windows. The major

energy-use _____ problems will be identified, and

_____ analyst will recommend _____

ways to use _____ energy more efficiently.

Fill in the blanks with the correct article. If no article is required, write an X in the blank.

Example Paragraph 16

_____ Great Teacher

To this day, I am completely convinced that _____ main reason that I did so well in my French class in _____ high school was the incredible teacher that I had, _____ Mrs. Montluzin. I had not studied _____ foreign language before I started _____ Mrs. Montluzin's French class. _____ idea of being able to communicate in a foreign language, especially _____ French, intrigued me, but _____ idea also scared me. _____ French seemed so difficult at first. We had so much _____ vocabulary to memorize, and we had to do _____ exercises to improve our grammar. While it is true that there was _____ great deal of work to do, _____ Mrs. Montluzin always tried her best to make French class very interesting. She also gave us _____ suggestions for learning _____ French, and these helped me a lot. Since this French class, I have studied a few other languages, and my interest in _____ foreign languages today is due to _____ success I had in French class with _____ Mrs. Montluzin.

ACTIVITY 10

Fill in the blanks with the correct article. If no article is required, write an X in the blank.

Example Paragraph 17

_____ Surprising Statistics on _____ Higher Education in _____ United States

Although _____ United States is a leader in many areas, it is surprising that _____ number of Americans with _____ college degree is not as high as it is in some _____ other countries. Only about 22 percent of

_____ Americans have attended college for four or more

years. To _____ most people, this rather low ratio of one

in five is shocking. Slightly more than _____ 60 percent

of _____ Americans between _____

ages of 25 and 40 have taken some _____ college classes.

Though these numbers are far from what _____ many

people would expect in _____ United States, these

statistics are _____ huge improvement over figures

at _____ turn of _____ last century.

In _____ 1900, only about _____ 8

percent of all Americans even entered _____ college. At

_____ present time, there are about 21 million students

attending _____ college.

Editing for Errors

ACTIVITY 11

This paragraph contains eight errors. They are in word choice (one), article (one), modal* (one), verb tense (one), subject-verb agreement (three), and word order (one). Mark these errors and write the corrections above the errors.

Example Paragraph 18

A Dangerous Driving Problem

Imagine that you are driving your car home from mall or the library. You come to a bend in the road. You decide that you need to slow down a little, so you tap the brake pedal. Much to your surprise, the car does not begin to slow down. You push the brake pedal all the way down to the floor, but still anything happens. There are a few things you can do when your brakes does not work. One was to pump the brakes. If also this fails, you should to try the emergency brake. If this also fail, you should try to shift the car into a lower gear and rub the tires against the curb until the car come to a stop.

*Modals are *can, should, will, must, may,* and *might.* Modals appear before verbs. We do not use *to* between modals and verbs. *(Incorrect:* I should to go with him. *Correct:* I should go with him.) Modals do not have forms that take *-s, -ing,* or *-ed.*

This paragraph contains ten errors. They are in prepositions (three), word order (one), articles (two), and verb tense (four). Mark these errors and write the corrections above the errors.

The Start of My Love of Aquariums

My love of aquariums began a long time ago. Although I got my first fish when I am just seven years old, I can still remember the store, the fish, and salesclerk who waited on me that day. Because I made good grades on my report card, my uncle has rewarded me with a dollar. A few days later, I was finally able to go to the local dime store for spend my money. It was 1965, and dollar could buy a lot. I looked a lot of different things, but I finally chose to buy a fish. We had an old fishbowl at home, so it seems logical with me to get a fish. I must have spent 15 minutes pacing back and forth in front of all the aquariums before I finally choose my fish. It was a green swordtail, or rather, she was a green swordtail. A few weeks later, she gave birth to 20 or 30 baby swordtails. Years later, I can still remember the fish beautiful that got me so interested in aquariums.

This paragraph contains eight errors. They are in prepositions (one), articles (three), word forms (two), verb tense (one), and subject-verb agreement (one). Mark these errors and write the corrections above the errors.

An Effect of Cellphones on Drivers

Cellular phones, can be threat to safety. A recent study for Donald Redelmeier and Robert Tibshirani of the University of Toronto showed that cellular phones pose a risk to drivers. In fact, people who talk on the phone while driving are four time more likely to have an automobile accident than those who do not use the phone while drive. The Toronto researchers studied 699 drivers who had been in an automobile accident while they were using their cellular phones. The researchers concluded that the main reason for the accidents is not that people used one hand for the telephone and only one for driving. Rather, cause of the accidents was usually that the drivers became distracted, angry, or upset by the phone call. The drivers then lost concentration and was more prone to a car accident.

This paragraph contains seven errors. They are in verb tense (one), articles (two), word forms (three), and subject-verb agreement (one). Mark these errors and write the corrections.

Example Paragraph 21

Problems with American Coins

Many foreigners who come to the United States have very hard time getting used to America coins. The denominations of the coins are one, five, ten, 25, and 50 cents, and one dollar. However, people used only the first four regularly. The smallest coin in value is the penny, but it is not the smallest coin in size. The quarter is one-fourth the value of a dollar, but it is not one-fourth as big as a dollar. There is a dollar coin, but no one ever use it. In fact, perhaps the only place to find one is at a bank. All of the coins are silver-colored except for one, the penny. Finally, because value of each coin is not clearly written on the coin as it is in many country, foreigners often experience problems with monetarily transactions.

ACTIVITY 15

This paragraph contains seven errors. They are in word order (one), articles (two), preposition (one), subject-verb agreement (one), and verb tense (two). Mark these errors and write the corrections.

Example Paragraph 22

An Oasis of Silence

Life on this campus can be extremely hectic, so when I want the solitude, I go usually to the fourth floor of the library. The fourth floor has nothing but shelves and shelves of rare books and obscure periodicals. Because there are only a few small tables with some rather uncomfortable wooden chairs and no copy machines in this floor, few people are staying here very long. Students search for a book or periodical, found it, and then take it to a more sociable floor to photocopy the pages or simply browse through the articles. One of my best friends have told me that he does not like this floor that is so special to me. For him, it is a lonely place. For me, however, it is oasis of silence in a land of turmoil, a place where I can read, think, and write in peace.

Useful Vocabulary for Better Writing

These useful words and phrases can help you write better sentences and paragraphs. They can make your writing sound more academic, natural, and fluent.

Giving and Adding Examples

Words and Phrases	Examples
For example, S + V / *For instance,* S + V	Our reading teacher assigns a lot of homework. *For example,* last night we had to read ten pages and write an essay.
The first reason + VERB	The article we read in class gave three reasons that our planet is in trouble. *The first reason* is about the increasing population.

Concluding Sentences

Words and Phrases	Examples
In conclusion, S + V	*In conclusion,* I believe everyone should vote in every election.
By doing all of these things, S + V	*By doing all of these things,* we can improve education in our country.
Because of this, S + V	*Because of this,* many people will have better health care.
As a result, S + V	*As a result,* I chose to go to college in France instead of my country.
For these reasons, S + V	*For these reasons,* I prefer to eat at home instead of a restaurant.
In sum, S + V / *In summary,* S + V / *To summarize ,* S + V	*In sum,* World War II was a very complicated war with many countries fighting for very different reasons, but in many ways, it was a continuation of World War I.
In other words, S + V	*In other words,* the judge made an incorrect decision.
From the information given, we can conclude that S + V	*From the information given, we can conclude that* Mark Johnson is certainly the best soccer player in this decade.
It is clear that S + V	*It is clear that* exercising every day improved your health.

Comparing

Words and Phrases	Examples
NOUN *is* COMPARATIVE ADJECTIVE *than* NOUN	New York *is larger than* Rhode Island.
S + V + COMPARATIVE ADVERB *than* Y.	The cats ran *faster than* the dogs.
S + V. *In comparison,* S + V.	Canada has provinces. *In comparison,* Brazil has states.
Although NOUN *and* NOUN *are similar in* NOUN, S + V	*Although* France *and* Spain *are similar in* size, they are different in many ways.
NOUN *and* NOUN *are similar.*	Brazil *and* the United States *are* surprisingly *similar.*
NOUN *is the same*	Our house *is the same* size as your house.
…as ADJECTIVE *as…*	Our house is *as big as* your house.
Like NOUN, NOUN *also*	*Like* Brazil, Mexico *also* has states.
both NOUN *and* NOUN…	*In both* German *and* Japanese, the verb appears at the end of a sentence.

Likewise, S + V / Also, S + V	The blooms on the red roses last longer than most other flowers. *Likewise*, the blooms for the pink rose are long-lasting.
Similarly, S + V .../ Similar to NOUN	Economists believe India has a bright future. *Similarly*, Brazil's future is on a very positive track.

Contrasting

Words and Phrases	Examples
S + V. In contrast, S + V.	*Algeria* is a very large country. *In contrast*, the UAE is very small.
Contrasted with / In contrast to NOUN	*In contrast to* last year, our company has doubled its profits this year.
Although / Even though / Though S + V	*Although* Spain and France are similar in size, they are different in many other ways.
Unlike NOUN,	*Unlike* the pink roses, the red roses are very expensive.
However, S + V	Canada has provinces. *However*, Brazil has states.
On the one hand, S + V On the other hand, S + V	*On the one hand*, Maggie loved to travel. *On the other hand*, she hated to be away from her home.
The opposite S + V	Most of the small towns in my state are experiencing a boom in tourism. In my hometown, *the opposite* is true.
NOUN *and* NOUN *are different.*	My older brother *and* my younger brother *are very different.*

Telling a Story / Narrating

Words and Phrases	Examples
When I was X, I would VERB	*When I was* a child, *I would* go fishing every weekend.
I have never felt so ADJ in my life.	*I have never felt so* anxious *in my life.*
I will never forget NOUN	*I will never forget* the day I took my first international flight.
I can still remember NOUN / I will always remember NOUN	*I can still remember* the day I started my first job.
NOUN *was the best / worst day of my life.*	My wedding was *the best day of my life.*
Every time X happened, Y happened.	*Every time* I used that computer, I had a problem.
This was my first ...	*This was my first* job after graduating from college.

Describing a Process

Words and Phrases	Examples
First (Second, Third, etc.), ... Next,... After that,...Then,... Finally,...	*First,* I cut the apples into small pieces. *Next,* I added some mayonnaise. *After that,* I added some salt. *Finally,* I mixed everything together well.
The first thing you should do is VERB	*The first thing you should do is* turn on the computer.
VERB+-ing requires you to follow (number) of steps.	*Saving* a file on a computer *requires you to follow several simple steps.*
Before you VERB, you should VERB.	*Before you* write a paragraph, *you should* brainstorm for ideas.
After (When)...	*After* you brainstorm your ideas, you can select the best ones to write about in your essay.

After that, …	After that, you can select the best ones to write about in your essay.
The last step is… / Finally, …	Finally, you should cook all of the ingredients for an hour.
If you follow these important steps in VERB + -ing,…	If you follow these important steps in applying for a passport, you will have your new document in a very short time.

Defining

Words and Phrases	Examples
The NOUN, which is a/an NOUN + ADJECTIVE CLAUSE, MAIN VERB	An owl, which is a bird that has huge round eyes, is awake most of the night.
According to the dictionary…	According to The Collins Cobuild Dictionary of American English, gossip is "an informal conversation, often about people's private affairs."
The dictionary definition of NOUN	The dictionary definition of gumbo is not very good.
X released a report stating that S + V	The president's office released a report stating that the new law will require all adults between the ages of 18 and 30 to serve at least one year of active military duty.
In other words, S + V	In other words, we have to redo everything we have done so far.
,…which means…	The paper is due tomorrow, which means if you want to get a good grade, you need to finish it today.
NOUN means…	Gossip means talking or writing about other people's private affairs.

Showing Cause and Effect

Words and Phrases	Examples
Because of NOUN, S + V. Because S + V, S + V.	Because of the traffic problems, it is easy to see why the city is building a new tunnel.
NOUN can trigger NOUN. NOUN can cause NOUN.	An earthquake can trigger tidal waves and can cause massive destruction.
Due to NOUN, …	Due to the snowstorm, all schools will be closed tomorrow.
As a result of NOUN…	As a result of his efforts, he got a better job.
Therefore,…/ As a result,…/ For this reason,…/ Consequently,…	It suddenly began to rain. Therefore, we all got wet.
NOUN will bring about …	The use of the Internet will bring about a change in education.
NOUN has had a good / bad effect on…	Computer technology has had both positive and negative effects on society.
The correlation is clear / evident.	The correlation between junk food and obesity is clear.

Describing

Words and Phrases	Examples
Prepositions of location: *above, across, around, in the dark, near, under…*	The children raced their bikes *around* the school.
Descriptive adjectives: *wonderful, delightful, dangerous, informative, rusty…*	The *bent, rusty* bike squeaked when I rode it.
SUBJECT *is* ADJECTIVE.	This dictionary *is informative*.
X is the most ADJECTIVE + NOUN.	To me, Germany *is the most interesting* country in Europe.
X tastes / looks / smells / feels like NOUN.	My ID card *looks like* a credit card.
X is known / famous for its NOUN.	France *is known for* its cheese.

Stating an Opinion

Words and Phrases	Examples
Without a doubt, VERB *is* ADJECTIVE *idea / method / decision / way.*	*Without a doubt,* walking to work each day *is* an excellent *way* to lose weight.
Personally, I believe/think/feel/agree/ disagree/ suppose S + V.	*Personally, I believe that* smoking on a bus should not be allowed.
VERB+-*ing should not be allowed.*	Smoking in public *should not be allowed.*
In my opinion/ view/ experience, NOUN	*In my opinion,* smoking is rude.
For this reason, S + V. / *That is why I think…*	I do not have a car. *For this reason,* I do not care about rising gasoline prices.
There are many benefits / advantages to NOUN.	*There are many benefits* to swimming every day.
There are many drawbacks / disadvantages to NOUN.	*There are many drawbacks* to eating your meals at a restaurant.
I am convinced that S + V	*I am convinced that* education at a university should be free to all citizens.
NOUN *should be required / mandatory.*	College *should be required.*
I prefer NOUN *to* NOUN.	*I prefer* soccer to football.
To me, banning / prohibiting NOUN *makes (perfect) sense.*	*To me, banning* cell phones while driving *makes perfect sense.*
For all of these important reasons, I think / believe / feel (that) S + V	*For all of these important reasons, I think* smoking *should be* banned in public.
Based on X, I have come to the conclusion that S + V	*Based on* two books that I read recently, *I have come to the conclusion that* global warming is the most serious problem that my generation faces.

Arguing and Persuading

Words and Phrases	Examples
It is important to remember that S + V	*It is important to remember* that school uniforms would only be worn during school hours.
According to a recent survey, S + V	*According to a recent survey,* 85 percent of high school students felt they had too much homework.
Even more important, S + V	*Even more important,* statistics show the positive effects that school uniforms have on behavior.
Despite this, S + V	The report says this particular kind of airplane is dangerous. *Despite this,* the government has not banned this airplane.
SUBJECT *must / should / ought to* VERB	Researchers *must* stop unethical animal testing.
The reason for S + V	*The reason for* people's support of this plan is that it provides equal treatment for all citizens.
To emphasize, S + V	*To emphasize,* I support a lower age for voting but only for those who already have a high school diploma.
For these reasons, S + V	*For these reasons,* public schools should require uniforms.
Obviously, S + V	*Obviously,* there are many people who would disagree with what I have just said.
Without a doubt, S + V	*Without a doubt,* students ought to learn a foreign language.
I agree that S + V. *However* S + V	*I agree that* a college degree is important. *However,* getting a practical technical license can also be very useful.

Reacting/Responding

Words and Phrases	Examples
TITLE *by* AUTHOR *is a / an…*	*Harry Potter and the Goblet of Fire* by J.K. Rowling *is an* entertaining book to read.
My first reaction to the prompt / news / article was / is NOUN.	*My first reaction to the article was* fear.
When I read / look at / think about NOUN, *I was amazed / shocked / surprised …*	*When I read* the article, *I was surprised* to learn of his athletic ability.

NOTES

NOTES

NOTES

NOTES

NOTES

NOTES

NOTES